# A World Within

## Spiritual Awakening in Modern Times

CRAIG BRUCE

iUniverse, Inc.
New York Bloomington

# A World Within
## Spiritual Awakening in Modern Times

*iUniverse books may be ordered through booksellers or by contacting:*

*iUniverse*
*1663 Liberty Drive*
*Bloomington, IN 47403*
*www.iuniverse.com*
*1-800-Authors (1-800-288-4677)*

*Because of the dynamic nature of the Internet, any Web addresses or links contained in this book may have changed since publication and may no longer be valid. The views expressed in this work are solely those of the author and do not necessarily reflect the views of the publisher, and the publisher hereby disclaims any responsibility for them.*

*ISBN: 978-1-4401-5678-6 (pbk)*
*ISBN: 978-1-4401-5679-3 (ebook)*

*Printed in the United States of America*

*iUniverse rev. date:9/2/09*

To Jeremy and Alex for sharing the wonder and mystery of our lives, woven together in this experience.

For as long as I could remember, my experience of life had often been a feeling of dangling from the edge of a cliff by the tips of my fingers, anxious and alone. Only recently did I realize that, all along, the safety and stability of the ground were never more than an inch below my feet …

# Contents

# Preface

> To thine own self be true. And it must follow, as
> the night the day, Thou canst not then be false to
> any man.                    —*William Shakespeare*

The notion of writing a book had never occurred to me until
I began to understand that I was in the middle of a spiritual
awakening. During my four decades on earth, I had always taken
for granted that true spiritual experiences didn't happen to people
like me: a middle-aged, professional, family man pursuing the
American dream—a nice Jewish boy who had never been very
religious. When I became involved in meditation, I thought I was
engaging in a novel method of relaxation to help reduce stress in
my daily life. I didn't understand that I had really embarked on
a spiritual quest. I didn't know that I was actually making direct
contact with the part of me that is infinite.

As you will see shortly, my early glimpses of Spirit started an
odyssey that changed my life and dramatically altered my view
of the universe. Along the way, I also realized four important
things.

- One was how much more there was to me than I had ever
  imagined.
- Another was that all human beings are on their own spiritual
  odysseys right now, and there is much more to them, too.
  However, most are not conscious of this fact.

- Related to this idea was the realization that we, as a race of humans, are waking up at an accelerating pace, meaning that many more of us will now be having similar experiences than ever before.

- Finally, I discovered the truth in the old saying that once you awaken spiritually, you can't turn back. Indeed, I tried to abandon my journey at one point, with shocking consequences, and even then found that my desire to know more would not be denied.

I ended up devoting several years to exploring wisdom from many diverse spiritual and scientific sources, looking for a context in which to comprehend this stirring of numinous inspiration. As time passed, I realized that this spiritual quest had enriched my life immeasurably and that I needed to share what I had found. All my searching convinced me that a practical guide to help others explore this immense territory was vitally needed. A clear explanation of what it means to awaken spiritually in contemporary society is essential today, not only from the vantage point of an established spiritual master or expert, but also through the eyes of a regular person like me who can speak from this level of understanding. A book such as this one will be a valuable resource for the many who now realize that they, too, are traveling along the road to their own spiritual self-discovery, but who haven't yet found a down-to-earth introduction that shows them where to find the on-ramps and detours.

> Empowering yourself to discover who you truly are is your highest pursuit in life.

*A World Within* will help you look beyond the boundaries of your preexisting beliefs for personal freedom and the self-empowerment it can bring. It is not widely known, but "30–40 percent of the population have had mystical experiences."*,[1] These extraordinary events can upset one's balance

---

* Though at the same time, "only 19 percent of adult Americans regularly practice their religion."

in our outwardly oriented society. Yet they are becoming more frequent, precisely because conventional assumptions about existence no longer seem to work in a world of accelerating speed, complexity, and turmoil. Increasingly, more people yearn to reconnect to the sacred and feel a call to look inward for their essential identity. Perhaps you are one in whom the need for a truly felt spirituality is now emerging. If so, *A World Within* will acquaint you with the terrain of spiritual awakening in the modern world. You will find a simple way to practice, to get right to the heart of inviting direct experience, instead of following a set of barren concepts or externally imposed requirements. As you awaken, you will receive the continuing support and guidance you need, in practical ways, to incorporate your changing perspectives into your everyday life for greater fulfillment.

Think of this book as an exploration of a very large spiritual house with many different rooms. So much wonderful (as well as questionable) material exists about each of these rooms that my goal is certainly not to redecorate them, so to speak. My intent is to provide four distinct but related tours of this house to serve as an effective starting point for you to explore the different rooms further. The tours I have created are as follows:

- **Personal Experience and Insights**
  As I have mentioned, I relate my story to give you a sense of what it's like for an average person to begin a spiritual awakening. Of course, everyone is different and no two paths are the same, but a commonality of experience has always existed across all peoples through the centuries. I have discovered, from many diverse sources, that the basic features of my awakening aren't much different from this shared understanding. The features of your awakening should not be dissimilar, either.

  My story will offer you a particularly beneficial perspective because it unfolded right in the middle of my modern, workaday existence in the suburbs of a major American city.

More importantly, my inner odyssey continues today, even as I maintain my external way of life. I have been greatly inspired by the wonderful wisdom of gifted teachers and writers like Jack Kornfield and Caroline Myss.* But, unlike them, I did not devote most of my life to spiritual practice or face the need to harness a highly developed spiritual talent. I suspect that most people who are beginning their search for meaning are coming from ordinary circumstances akin to mine.

What you will understand is that spiritual growth usually doesn't follow a predictable pattern, like a graph always going up and to the right, with divine bliss increasing in a never-ending progression. There are also quiet periods of assimilation, periods of rapidly changing energy, difficult choices to make, and times when you question what you thought you were already sure of knowing. But then, you discover that no matter what happens, the peace and bliss are always there, always waiting to be allowed in. It's a process, one that really never ends, but one that you get the hang of after a while. In the introduction and Chapters 1 through 4, I give you my personal background and then describe what happened to me beginning in early 1999.

It seemed natural to follow my experience with the insights I gained, as a result, about the process of spiritual awakening (Chapter 5, Walking the Talk). Now clear to me is that this process has many different attributes, the knowing of which could be very helpful to people trying to find their way in the world today. Love is the most important of these attributes, and I fully explore its central role in furthering spiritual development through the release of fear. I also establish a strategy for practicing spiritual growth that considers the

---

\* Kornfield was a Buddhist monk who lived and trained in Southeast Asia for many years; he is also a Western psychologist. Myss is a medical intuitive who has the ability to diagnose, sometimes from a remote location, the medical problems of others before they manifest physically.

challenges of modern living, as well as the ups and downs inherent in the process. This chapter presents specific ways that demonstrate how you can more comfortably integrate into your life your evolving perspectives. Most of them are well documented in the published material I have examined (see the Conceptual Guide in Chapter 9), but it occurred to me that a readily understandable overview with pointers on where to go for more information seemed to be lacking. I fill that gap with the added dimension of the perspective I gained from having to find my own way.

A logical extension of sharing my insights on spiritual growth is my attempt to summarize the foundational Reality upon which everything is built (Chapter 6, The Bigger Picture). This macro view of spirituality begins with a description of the contours of existence and shows them to be much grander than those embodied by conventional perceptions, beliefs, or doctrine. These ideas are then contrasted with what our deeply held religious and cultural frameworks usually tell us about the human condition. The differences are clear, and from these, we can see that spiritual awakening on a personal level is really where the knowledge and experience of reality becomes available to the world at large. Because of the obvious vastness of this subject, I came to appreciate that an overview of the recurring themes across all of the published material would be essential to anyone needing to get the basics in one place.

- **Experiential Guide**
  The only way you will become conscious of who you really are is simply to do it. I have found meditating a very effective way to reach the point of stillness where I can encounter what is real. Innumerable paths exist to reach the divinity within, and there are many ways to meditate, all waiting for you to discover, if you wish.

  What's always been fascinating to me about the method

I use is that, basically, I made it up as I went along. To be sure, I read many books and absorbed lots of information that contributed to how I practice. But I had no teacher or system, which proves to me that the only thing anyone really needs is genuineness of purpose. There is no *right* way to gain access to what is inherently yours. My method is very simple, yet effective. In Chapter 7, I present this easy-to-follow meditation program, as well as an overview of other experiential practices.

- **Cautionary Considerations**
  No exploration of the process of spiritual awakening would be complete without an honest look at some of the more significant areas of discomfort that may arise occasionally. I believe that three of these areas are particularly important to anyone desiring a more comprehensive picture that includes the challenges possible along the way. They are the role of spiritual teachers as a catalyst to spiritual growth, the conditions of spiritual emergency and its treatment, and the use of psychoactive drugs to accelerate spiritual illumination. In Chapter 8, I have drawn from some of my personal experience, as well as several sources that give valuable, in-depth information on these subjects. While the spiritual path is not always smooth, it always helps to know as much as possible about the terrain.

- **Conceptual Guide**
  Here is where I summarize a lot of the wonderful published information that is available. Many more resources exist, of course, but this guide gives you a wide-ranging palette of spiritual color to explore. An amazing consistency permeates this material, even though it comes through so many different cultures, personalities, and even dimensions. It's just a matter of deciding what language rings true for you.
  
  The other amazing aspect is that this wisdom is available

at all. Up until the last three decades or so, for thousands of years, only high priests, yogis, monks, and shamans were privy to this knowledge. It's a wonder that it's coming out of the woodwork suddenly after all this time. I also review scientific resources that help demonstrate the way even our physical understanding of the universe is converging around many of the same mysteries. The only material not included is that from the mainstream religions, since so many people are already grounded in some form of religious system. Naturally, sincere practice of a religion's core teachings of love can open your eyes, too. Note: At certain points in the book, I have included the numbered references to the sources reviewed in Chapter 9 as citations to indicate where I believe you may find it important to explore a particular concept more deeply.

**Terminology and Usage**
Let's consider a few more ideas before we begin. In certain places, you will see words such as *Reality, Truth, Love*, and *Universe* beginning with a capital letter. In these instances, it was my intention to refer to their ultimate or true nature (e.g., Reality, as it exists in the absolute). You will see that using any of these terms in this way is really the same as referring to God. When these words begin in lowercase, individual perception enters the picture so that reality could mean my view, or your view, of what is still the One Reality that is actually present.

Other points of usage I should explain concern the terms *ego, spirituality, God,* and *Divine Love.*

• Here, ego refers to the ingrained personal beliefs and habits that collectively constitute an illusory sense of self and the main barrier to the greater awareness of all there truly is to experience. In conventional terms, the ego is viewed as the part of the psyche that actually is the apparent self and which deals with the external world as sensed through waking levels

of awareness. I make this distinction not to invalidate the
need for a healthy ego to experience physical reality, but to
bring to light the fact that a dominant ego obscures the rest
of the self, of which it is only a small piece.

- By spirituality, I simply mean the direct knowing of one's
Essence, Soul, or Divine Being. The spiritual path is one of self-
discovery, the knowing, little by little, of the Self as infinite, as
well as specific. I am not referring to the doctrine or codes of
morality that the words *religion* and *faith* commonly suggest
and which have become largely the domain of the ego. At the
same time, I do recognize that encounters of a Divine nature
within a traditional religious system are possible and valid.

- Closely connected to spirituality in this context is the idea
of God as Universal Mind or Cosmic Intelligence in which
the natural and perpetual unfolding of everything seen and
unseen occurs. God, as the Source of All That Is, exists in
a singular state of absolute perfection, but continually
creates infinite realms of duality and units of consciousness,
including Humans Beings, to have the unending experiential
knowledge of Itself.

- Accordingly, Divine Love is the true state in which All
That Is unfolds. It is a much richer, all-encompassing,
and less-personalized Love than is known through its
earthly counterparts—romance, interpersonal caring, great
adoration, and the like—although earthly love ultimately
has its source in Divine Love. Again, these experiential views
are in contrast to the more conventional religious definitions
having their basis in law or belief. I will explore these ideas
more fully later.

**Reducing My Experience to Words**

I also need to mention the difficulty of putting subjective
experiences, especially those not commonly understood, into
words. This, of course, is an age-old problem and the main reason
metaphors and parables exist. As Albert Einstein explained, "It is

very difficult to elucidate [cosmic religious] feeling to anyone who is entirely without it, especially as there is no anthropomorphic* conception of God corresponding to it." Even so, I have tried hard to find the right words to convey the meaning and knowing I felt, in spite of realizing that words can only go so far. My purpose was to give you the flavor of what is possible, describe how such experiences feel, and, hopefully, arouse your curiosity to explore this territory for yourself.

I faced some personal challenges, too. One was the idea of exposing my life story, aware that the whole world would see it. Not many people I meet on a daily basis know my background this intimately, and many will be very surprised to see me writing on the subject of spiritual awakening. Some may be upset by my views. Some may even think that I have lost my mind. On the other hand, those who have known me to be a rather rational person might conclude that there must be at least a grain of truth to all of this and that I really am just reporting events that actually happened. Although daunting, these concerns were not enough to deter me. Besides, as I said, my history and what I am seeking aren't very different from many of you reading this right now.

Finally, I wrestled with the uncomfortable notion that some people may choose to see me in the role of a sage giving absolute answers when I know that I am simply speaking as one who is getting closer to knowing his own Truth. I can't know what is true for someone else, yet I am certain of my intent, that being to help others find their own answers in the only place they can be found, within themselves. So in spite of all my reservations, I have decided to let the chips fall where they may because, ultimately, there is no way I can avoid it.

---

\* A common anthropomorphic view of Universal Intelligence found in most religions is the conception of God as a male being who reacts with the human emotion of anger when His laws are broken.

# Introduction

Do you recognize the bell of truth when you hear
it ring?
—*Leon Russell, from his song, "Stranger in a Strange
Land"*

I don't consider myself a master or a guru, but I do know that
every one of us is traveling the path to spiritual mastery, regardless
of whether we are aware of it. How do I know? In 1999, during
my early forties, I had what I will call a spiritual awakening.
Unexpectedly, I began to have direct experiences of an intensely
spiritual nature. Please don't associate these events with religion
or doctrine of any kind. As of this writing, I have not joined any
group or formally sought any personal spiritual advice in such a
setting (not that I wouldn't do so if it became appropriate).

But, I did realize that if this could happen to me, it could
happen to anyone. As such, I felt it would be helpful for others
to hear about my personal adventure, one that I now realize is
only beginning to unfold. I also needed to create for those who
knew me well, and who saw me change for no apparent reason,
the means to someday understand what had happened to me. I
have found it close to impossible to explain my experience in
conversation; I hope that taking the time to articulate it in writing
will prove more effective. As much as anything, though, I needed
an outlet for all that was welling up inside me for some time.

Thus, for therapeutic reasons, and to try to get my arms around everything that has happened, this endeavor became a necessity.

Since my awakening, I have traveled this path alone, with just my intuition and intellect as my guides. The only external influences have been from published

> A much bigger picture exists than what is usually evident in physical reality, and things are not always as they seem.

information, some of which you will find in the Conceptual Guide to spiritual and scientific wisdom (Chapter 9). As I indicate later, this material resonated with me because it put into context the spiritual experiences I was already having, and, at the bottom line, it promoted a completely sane picture of the universe, one of love and order, and individual power and freedom.

Internally, my direct experiences have shown me that a much bigger picture exists than what is usually evident in physical reality and that things are not always as they seem. These have profoundly increased my awareness of what is truly important in life and the value in taking up the struggle to consciously and continually expand and refine the concept of who I am. They have demonstrated to me that, as a Human Being, I have tremendous energy available to me, almost all of which I had been expending on unquestioned assumptions about reality and what some call self-importance (or self-absorption). By the conscious practice of releasing negativity and ego attachments over time, more energy became available to me to expand my spiritual awareness. As this virtuous circle gained momentum, I found myself more often having a profound inner peace and security that allowed me to see the world in ways previously not available to me.

That is not to say that any of this has been without challenges. After all, I don't live in a vacuum; other people share my life, and the changes in me have caused them to change as well. It was difficult, and still is at times, for those with whom I am closest to accept the new me. Situations that always had elicited the same reactions were no longer predictable. There was a period of adjustment during which my family seemed to fear that my diminishing worry about the future, for instance, meant that they could no longer depend on me. Lifestyle and character adjustments, such as my decision not to eat meat or my newfound willingness to question cherished beliefs and definitions of propriety, raised more than a few eyebrows and questions about what had gotten into me.

All of this was very troubling to people who had relied on me to be their rock in a complex world, especially when they had no idea what I was going through, and I had no words to adequately explain it. However, my family has experienced a benefit that far outweighs their feelings of insecurity, at least in my view. I believe I am setting an example that will help them someday when they decide to wake up. Every day they see me consciously striving to do the best I can. They see me meditating and taking care of my body, becoming a vegetarian (on principle, not just for health reasons), avoiding ego dramas with others, and trying to frame every decision I make in a larger context. They may roll their eyes and say I am being ridiculous, or even express outright disapproval, but I know that somewhere down the line, they will all wrestle with the same issues and questions. As an aside, it's ironic that not long after I had my initial awakening, I was promoted to a director level position in my company. I am certain that my newfound inner peace allowed for this to happen and that the "old me" could not have handled the increased responsibility.

The other major challenge for me has been that spiritual opening is not a linear process and is not always blissful and rapturous. In fact, early on, I was frightened and confused at times. My glimpses of the Divine included what I can only describe as a powerful, electric-like energy running through my body, and, sometimes, I felt that I was close to passing on. Most terrifying was actually a period when I experienced Divine Love so incredibly intense that I thought my identity would completely disintegrate. When, in fear, I turned away from this love, I found myself hanging on to my sanity by a thread, literally standing at the edge of an abyss that was all too real to me. On the two occasions when this happened, it took me days to fully recover. At other times, I felt my physiology changing, and I would have almost no energy the next day.

More mundane problems include hiding my true feelings and editing my words with almost everyone, knowing that they were not congruent with our culture's prevailing worldview. I have seldom had opportunities to share any of my experiences or perspectives with those who would understand them. The few times I have tested the water with neighbors or people at work (almost always in response to a conversation they have initiated), it quickly becomes apparent that my outlook is substantially different. Some exceptions happen, fortunately. My sister, cousins, fiancée, and a good friend have each been there for me to talk to and while they don't necessarily identify with my views yet, they are at least are open-minded enough to listen.

In fairness to those around me, perhaps some of my reticence has been due to confusion on my part. I still live in the material world as everybody else does, but at times, it can be uncomfortable when (I assume) I am the only one seeing it through a spiritual lens. Yet I often sense some of my co-workers, friends, and family searching for the same thing I am beginning to find. It does get frustrating dancing around what is now so obvious to me instead of simply just stating it. Maybe that's part of the function of this book, to come out with it. After searching for more information and wisdom as I have described, I now know that this is all as it should be. And, I will face more challenges as I continue to wake up and change, but I can't turn back now—nor do I want to go back.

The fact that I suddenly began to wake up is all the evidence I need to know that awakening is happening everywhere. That gives me great hope for the planet. Like me, once you remember what you have really always known, you will be filled with awe and wonder, as well as a familiarity that you can't explain. Exploring your spiritual reality will become a great adventure that no one else can experience in your uniquely individual way. Your ego orientation of *I'll believe it when I see it* will change to a spiritual one of *I'll see it when I believe it.*

# Chapter 1

## The Road to Awakening

*The most beautiful experience we can have is the mysterious … the fundamental emotion which stands at the cradle of true art and true science.*
—*Albert Einstein*

For most of my forty-three years, until 1999, I had led a fairly unremarkable life. My experiences included deep loss (the death of my father when I was thirteen and my mother when I was twenty-nine) and great joy (my marriage and the birth of my two sons), but I would not consider these highs and lows to be unusual, all things considered. I am well educated, in good health, have done well professionally and, in the context of modern American society, I have been reasonably successful. Physically and materially, life had been pretty good.

I was born and raised as a member of the conservative branch of Judaism and received its requisite religious education, although neither of my parents practiced or approached our religion in a conscientious manner. My mom and dad were middle-class American Jews who were highly ethical and honorable, but who made no pretense of righteousness or piety. They each had an irreverent sense of humor, which I'm sure they didn't realize had rubbed off on me. I can remember them at the synagogue during services when I was about eleven years old, trying hard to stifle their laughter during a solemn moment, no doubt observing something totally inappropriate but genuinely funny. My parents gave my younger sister and me many gifts, the most precious being the inner certainty that we were loved. However, a strong grounding in our religion was not among them.

Many members of my extended family, however, were, and still are, highly observant. While growing up, it seemed to me that that they always knew the correct way to conduct the proceedings during High Holiday celebrations and Passover Seders, which were usually held at their houses. Now, looking back, I have fond memories of these family gatherings, but at the time, I could not deny vague feelings of not measuring up. In our home, the affinity for the traditions, an intuitive understanding of the laws and historic commentary, or a facility reading Hebrew were not remotely as strong as in their homes. I think that because I was aware of this contrast over the years I came to an unarticulated belief that my parents, and my sister and me, by extension, must have been lacking in some important way.

At various times during my life, I would try very hard in synagogue to experience the same spiritual revelations that some of my uncles, aunts, cousins, and the other devout congregants must have been encountering. To my way of thinking, a person who would earnestly pursue reading the Torah and practicing as a Jew must be doing it for truly spiritual reasons. To me, this meant finding and manifestly feeling the presence of God, not only being together among friends and family to recite prayers and observe rituals, however comforting these traditions may be. I don't mean to imply that my relatives were not finding God, only that I was not.

## Where's the Beef?

So, as I got older the question for me became, as an old Wendy's commercial once asked, "Where's the beef?" When I explored and compared the world's religions, I found that other faiths gave more voice to the question of spirit, especially as it concerned eternal life. Christianity featured a state of perfection called Heaven, but extremely rigorous requirements seemed necessary to get there, and everlasting damnation in hell if the requirements were not met. Islam struck me as exceedingly harsh, after hearing about the draconian punishments meted out in theocratic countries to those who broke the laws. The Eastern religions were the closest to describing eternity in a nonthreatening way, particularly through the principle of reincarnation. But, even there, the requirement to pay off karmic debts from the past to become enlightened seemed punitive.

In contrast to the other faiths, I gained an appreciation of Judaism's more humanistic approach to life's problems. The focus of Judaism, if I may put it this simply, is to live in harmony among one's community by following the 613 mitzvot, or commandments of the Torah. These laws are often thought of in a general sense, as the way to live righteously and justly, but they are actually an integral part of all facets of life including marriage, commerce and agriculture, for example. By continually performing mitzvot one maintains his or her connection to God and ultimately helps to heal the world. The mystical branch of Judaism, Kabbalah, calls this Tikkun ha-olam, collecting and reunifying the divine sparks that were scattered asunder when the earth was created. In any event, following the mitzvot is ultimately the way to know God in Judaism.

Unlike other religions, in Judaism, very little attention is given to what happens after death,* although, in typical fashion,

---

\*    Judaism does entertain the notion that a messiah will arrive (for the first time), raise the dead, and bring all who are righteous to God. The essence of this time could be characterized by Isaiah's prophecy that, "… nation shall not lift up sword against nation [and] neither shall they learn war anymore." Other conceptions and descriptions about what life after death would consist of are mainly from interpretations of the religious texts. However, in my experience attending services and other Jewish rites, most references to the afterlife are rather oblique, such as describing the soul's "going out and lots of commentary exists about the proper way to mourn or provide comfort to those who are grieving here on earth. Similarly, other than acknowledging the eternality of the soul, I have seen or heard nothing about one's existence before the current lifetime. Godliness in Judaism is found more in solving ethical problems in the world without much thought about what happens before or after this life. A person's eternal salvation, according to many other religions, in contrast, is dependent upon a personal battle waged against the forces of darkness and evil. Even the unimposing architecture of a synagogue reflects a more earthbound orientation to life in comparison to other houses of worship, with their spires, domes, and minarets soaring to heaven above.

Like other religions, Judaism does have some grave admonitions, such as the imperative to atone for the past year's sins so that one's name may be written into the Book of Life for the coming year. Also, many of the laws in the Torah are rooted in the cultural mores of three thousand years ago, and in some cases, they include harsh consequences for transgressors (death by stoning, for instance). Although most Jews today don't act on these laws literally, they do seek the meaning and intent of the Torah for guidance in daily living. A prolific collection of writings, known as the Talmud, containing centuries of debates on myriad subjects by the great rabbis is the main source of this guidance. In general, the three main branches of Judaism, Orthodox, Conservative, and Reform, differ primarily in their respective adherence to the letter of the law and willingness to modify religious practices as the world changes.

While I appreciated its humanism, I knew growing up that I

---

coming in" at funerals or conceiving the soul to be everlasting and forevermore in much of the liturgy. The following passage is an example: "With our lives we give life. Something of us can never die: we move in the eternal cycle of darkness and death, of light and life." This is a beautiful and moving sentiment, indeed, but one that only alludes to the full extent of human consciousness.

did not have the desire or stamina I needed to adhere to a sincere practice of Judaism, conservative or otherwise. The laws and stories in the Torah were fascinating, but I perceived the purpose of studying and following them only to be the satisfaction of obligations imposed by external authorities. On the level of deep spiritual feeling, try as I might, Judaism seemed to offer no transformational moments, at least not any that I recognized at the time. No prayer suddenly came to life, no sermon caused great understanding, and I never encountered evidence that I was anything other than my physical form having five built-in senses. The other religions did establish personal experience of the divine as a central article of faith, but their judgments, punishments, and apocalyptic visions were too fearsome for me to consider. Sometime during my thirties, I resigned myself to the apparent fact that the spiritual part of my life was dead, that this aspect of human experience was simply not available to me.

Intellectually, I considered myself to be open-minded as far as the universe was concerned. I believed that unexplained phenomena could be real and that the secular high priests of our society—scientists and doctors—could not explain, by any means, every aspect of reality. With all of the incredible complexity in nature, I considered God's existence to be inescapable. But, again, I had no direct, internal evidence of this truth.

Now, in the interest of full disclosure, I must convey that my father passed on not only just after my thirteenth birthday, but also on the day before my bar mitzvah. I offer this information for no other reason than because, some readers, upon learning about his death under these circumstances, may summarily attribute any of my subsequent religious belief and attitude

> All the events in one's life—the good and the bad—are there for our learning. From a larger perspective, there is no bad.

development mostly to this event. That this loss had a profound impact on my psychological state, relationships, and life in general is beyond question. Indeed, it was something I had to "dig out from under," so to speak. After all, the big celebration we had been anticipating and that was just twenty-four hours away instantly was reconfigured into a funeral.

Walking through the door after school, seeing my mother and our family doctor both crying, and absorbing what they were telling me is something I will never forget. My father suffered from emphysema and was not well, but we had no evidence of any immediate threat to his life. Suddenly, confusion erupted as urgent phone calls were made to dramatically change the plans of dozens of people. I remember numbly reading a book of John F. Kennedy's life in my bedroom to get from one moment to the next.

My bar mitzvah service was held ten days later at seven o'clock on a weekday morning and was truncated to less than a half hour. Yet, in hindsight, even with this trauma, I can honestly report no change in my religious or spiritual outlook. For a time, I begged God to bring my father back to me, but I never remember turning away from Judaism or turning toward another set of beliefs because of these events.

I have come to understand that all events in one's life—the good and the bad—are there for our learning. And, the events that we experience personally are woven together so that we also affect one another in a web of fantastic complexity, for reasons that are not always apparent at first. In fact, from a larger perspective there is no bad; even the so-called bad leads ultimately to greater awareness. But, I am getting ahead of myself.

**Searching and Drifting**
Later, as a teenager looking to fit in, I experimented with foreign ideas from time to time. Early in my high school career, I had two friends that were enamored with the philosophies of P.D. Ouspensky. In the early twentieth century, Ouspensky became well-known for his ideas on the evolution of man's consciousness and its relationship to the new physics that was then emerging. I read some of his works and tried to emulate my friends' passion

for this enlightening information; but, more than anything, I was merely going along for their acceptance. I certainly wasn't ready for this material at the time. I didn't even understand most of it.

Ideas weren't the only foreign things I experimented with during these years. After applying some intense peer pressure, the same friends convinced me to try marijuana. Initially, it was a different and exciting experience, heightened by my acceptance by guys who were actually a couple of years older, and therefore, supposedly wiser, than I was. Before long, though, smoking pot became a routine in my young life, anesthetizing me to my feelings and relationships with others. While I did not indulge frequently in more powerful drugs, including alcohol, I did partake of hallucinogens a few times (discussed later in Chapter 8, The Tao of Drugs). Even as I was choosing these activities, I knew deep inside that my pot smoking and forays into the world of psychedelic drugs were dead ends, and that I would eventually stop one day. That day came during my senior year in college when I had a large tumor removed from my trachea. The tumor proved benign, but the possibility that it could have turned out differently was the wake-up call I needed to let the marijuana go.

During the mid-1970s, as an undergraduate, I dabbled for about a month with a fundamentalist Christian group, attending a couple of their meetings. I had just read the book, *The Late, Great Planet Earth,* by Hal Lindsay, whose purpose was to map the prophecies of doom in the New Testament's Book of Revelation to then-current global events. This was a very powerful book, especially for an impressionable nineteen-year-old, and its primary effect was to scare the living daylights out of me. But, once I put the book aside and came to my senses, I lost interest in the group. I simply couldn't relate personally to its members, probably because they demonstrated no sense of humor and had no apparent interests besides their mission.

After college, as I entered the world of work and financial

responsibility, I developed strong opinions about lots of things, but had no real inner certainty to guide them. I adopted a fairly typical conservative worldview politically and economically, probably because it was congruent with the direction in which my life was moving. For many years, I had great debates on the issues of the day with my Uncle Monroe with whom I was very close (he passed on in 2000). His outlook on life was humanistic, gentle, and tolerant, which frustrated me. I saw him as being naïve in a world where power was the obvious answer to maintaining stability and where good and bad were intrinsically evident to any right-thinking person. Unlike me, however, my uncle did have a strong inner North Star* to guide him, as well as an equally formidable mind. His arguments were always logical, making subtle points that caught me off guard. I often found myself rebutting him in my thoughts later, so that I would be better prepared for the next time. But, the more I tried to convince him of the error of his beliefs, the more I became somehow unsure of my own. The subconscious doubts our conversations evoked in me ended up serving me well later on, and I am grateful for having had the benefit of his wisdom.

As I married and raised two sons through my thirties and early forties, I followed a lifestyle I imagine being quite typical in Western, especially American, society. The well-known pursuits of wealth accumulation and career advancement (which, by the way, I don't suggest even now are negative, in and of themselves) were my preoccupation. I went to synagogue sporadically and only to fulfill special obligations—bar mitzvahs, weddings, High Holidays, and the like.

In the meantime, I became so fixated on the daily detail of maintaining an external veneer that the scenery of my life was passing by without my awareness. Accomplishing tasks had

---

* Just as sailors since ancient times have relied on Polaris, the star that seems fixed directly above the North Pole, to find their bearings, so does one's inner sense of truth provide direction across the seas of life.

established itself as my main purpose, and I lived under this unarticulated mandate. I would tell myself, "If I can just finish these ten things, then I can enjoy myself," or rest, or whatever. Invariably, I never got to that place. I always had more tasks, more demands to keep the veneer looking good to the outside world, and more willingness on my part to keep turning up the speed on

> External experience and the enjoyment of it are part of our reason for being on earth. But, this is not, by any means, the only reason.

the proverbial treadmill. One summer, within a period of three months, I excavated a 150-foot drainage system in our yard by hand, replaced the walls and ceiling in our den, and installed a fence in the backyard. I did all of this with a full-time job during the day, graduate school at night, and a family in between.

It's clear to me now that I had reached a point that many, if not most of us, reach. Only, as in my case, we are not aware of it. We call this point falling asleep, becoming unconscious, or becoming totally identified with the ego. It's the unquestioning and unwitting identification with the external, meaning only what you can perceive through your physical senses. It's processing perceived information in a cursory manner, not giving any thought to your internal environment or intuition. It's the default acceptance of everything your parents, teachers, religious leaders, and culture tell you, and fear of the seemingly inherent consequences of challenging any of it.

## Looking in the Mirror

External experience and the enjoyment of it are part of our reason for being on earth. But, this is not, by any means, the only reason. As I found out there is so much more. Early in 1999 I began to feel a longing for something, but I could not put my finger on what it was. As I mentioned before, I was running at full speed through my life with my head down, looking only at the sidewalk and not noticing anything else around me. Then, seemingly out of nowhere, a new presence emerged. Suddenly, I had a consuming urge to change something, to do something drastic, to go in a different direction, but I didn't know where.

My job at this time was generating unusual stress for me. I had been heavily involved for the previous three years with a major information system project, and it was now going online. As with any large-scale project, unforeseen problems occurred. I was a key player in getting them resolved, while at the same time struggling to keep the company's operations running smoothly. I worked long hours filled with highly emotional people and frantic activity.

The system's material planning modules were not working properly, which meant that we could not determine with any confidence what parts to purchase for production. The only workaround was to do the calculations manually, a very laborious task, until the system was fixed. Since I was mainly responsible for implementing these modules, I was squarely on the hot seat. It took four months of troubleshooting the software to find a bug that had eluded us because the data and scenarios we used for testing were different in subtle ways from real-life operations. Perhaps this was the trigger that upset my internal apple cart. In any case, the longing I felt continued to get stronger. It became palpable, a visceral sensation, almost like being extremely thirsty, but more than that.

At first, I thought I was having a mid-life crisis of some sort. Perhaps, deep inside, I wanted to make up for some of those opportunities for fun and excitement I had missed earlier in life. After all, according to popular belief, I was at precisely the right age for these feelings. So, to try to sort things out, I made an appointment with a psychologist. To digress for a few moments, I had visited this therapist on a regular basis for most of my twenties to come to terms with pain I was feeling in relationships, of all types. I had friendships and romantic interests, but an all-pervading anxiety was constantly present in the background. I exerted a tremendous amount of energy worrying about others' opinions of me and building a façade of formidable intellectual power to mask my insecurity.

By the time I graduated college in 1977, I knew that my anxiety was only going to become more of a problem unless I did some serious self-analysis. My father's death eight years earlier had not only affected me deeply, but had affected my mother deeply as well. She had been seeing a psychologist during this time, and even in my teens, tried to persuade me to also visit this individual. Almost immediately upon returning home from school, I had one visit, then another, and soon began a nine-year journey into the realm of my psyche. I must say, I worked hard at this undertaking and took it very seriously, sometimes going twice per week for long stretches of time.

As for the psychologist, I cannot imagine a more skilled, patient, or completely honest therapist. It happened that my undergraduate degree was in psychology, so I was familiar with the various disciplines and approaches (e.g., Freudian, behavioral, humanistic, etc.). But, as the sessions progressed, it occurred to me that I could never identify any particular doctrine my therapist practiced. When I brought this to her attention, she would just say that she was in favor of whatever worked. And, indeed, she was adept at finding ways to hold a mirror to my mind, urging me to follow the threads of my anxieties back to their source.

The problem was that, for all of my willingness and her expert guidance, progress, although evident, was very slow and came in small increments. Every revelation would lead to two more questions or issues. It was as if I was playing a giant game of Whac-a-Mole in my head. While I had sessions that appeared to get down to bedrock issues, I could never seem to get the feeling of sustained progress—until I started to meditate.

One day in 1980 I was talking to a co-worker in the office. Somehow he started telling me about a Jose Silva book he had read, called *The Silva Mind Control Method*. This book, which I did not read until 1999, talks about the power of thought and visualization in creating one's physical reality. It also explains the role of meditation in facilitating this process. During my friend's discussion with me about this book, he described the way he meditated and the visualizations he did. Based solely on his verbal description, I became curious and decided to try it. At the time, I lived by myself in an apartment located close to work, an ideal situation where my time was my own and I had easy access to a secure and quiet environment. Every day, I would meditate for two twenty-minute periods, at home during lunch and again before dinner.

In a short time, probably two or three weeks, I began to get the hang of simply relaxing my body and clearing my mind, at least to a degree I hadn't realized was possible. Shortly thereafter, I seemed to reach a plateau where I usually attained a level of stillness and focus that was highly pleasing. At these times, I would experience deep relaxation within my hands, strangely enough, feeling as if they were floating in the air, unattached to my arms. But most interesting was that the feelings of relaxation soon began to carry over into my daily routine. I still felt negative emotions, such as anger, defensiveness, and the like, but I felt an element of detachment that had never existed before that time. It wasn't only that my emotions were attenuated to some degree; they increasingly became the subject of observation by another part of me. I was able to say, "Oh, this is anger," and recognize it internally as such, without having to expend nearly the same amount of energy to process it.

Most astounding to me was that these changes just happened. I had no intention or plan, much less any control over their emergence. Perhaps I had tapped into some unexplained process, maybe my subconscious, but the dramatic effects from meditating were in stark contrast to the incremental progress I had made during all my purposeful efforts in therapy. It wasn't long before my therapist detected the drop in my anxiety level and encouraged me to continue practicing the meditation, which I did for about a year.

Eventually, though, I became complacent and stopped

meditating. I can't say exactly why I stopped, but I think it was because I had reached that plateau and could not seem to go further. Maybe I was expecting to develop psychic abilities or have transformational experiences, and I became disappointed when they didn't happen. Also, it takes discipline to practice meditation consistently while the vagaries of life swirl about. On a bad day, it can be difficult to sit down and clear your inner space. In any event, I was choosing more and more to go to that movie or think about that problem at work rather than keep the twenty-minute appointments with myself.

Predictably, my anxiety level soon was back to where it had been. Nevertheless, I continued to work hard in therapy, gradually coming to a deeper understanding and acceptance of my emotions and personality nuances. In 1985, I accepted an assignment from my company to live in Japan for six months, a wonderful experience that greatly broadened my view of the world. I was responsible for helping to introduce an important new product into the Japanese market. This role provided me valuable business experience and the chance to form relationships with people in our international operations. I also took the opportunity for extensive personal travel, not only within Japan, but also across Southeast Asia and Australia. My adventures and exposure to other cultures during this period were certainly one of the high times of my life, and a great influence on me as well.

When I returned from my travels and resumed therapy, I found myself feeling much more unburdened and confident in general, and less motivated to continue the sessions. The goal my therapist and I had set for myself had always been, in a nutshell, to move past the anxiety so that I could have a more enjoyable experience of the world. Indeed, shortly after my return to the United States, I met my future wife, to whom I was married eight months later. My life became a whirlwind of changes as I moved in with my fiancée, acquired a new family of in-laws and new friends, and at the same time, managed my mother's affairs during her debilitating illness that soon ended with her passing.

Having successfully navigated these major events and milestones, my therapist and I agreed that I was ready to stop the sessions and get on with life.

The next thirteen years saw the birth of our two sons, two successive housing moves, a graduate degree, and increasing responsibility at work. Along with this came all of the attendant demands and activities of modern life that, as I described before, induced me to become further and further removed from a true sense of my self. All of which brings me back to the point of my mid-life crisis and the meeting with my old psychologist friend, whom I had not visited in thirteen years.

# Chapter 2

## I Am That

Awake, awake, your light has come! Arise, shine, awake and sing: the Eternal's glory dawns upon you.
—*Gates of Prayer (Reform Judaism Sabbath Prayer Book)[2]*

There are more things in heaven and earth, Horatio, Than are dreamt of in your philosophy.
—*William Shakespeare*

Stepping into her office, I immediately was at ease. I still felt that familiar feeling of having entered a haven, even if only for an hour, where I could talk to someone with complete openness about my trials and tribulations. Yet I discovered that a lot had changed, especially me. Perhaps because I had gotten along pretty well in the world without therapy for so long, I no longer felt the need for her support, or her approval. After some catching up, I proceeded to describe my current state of affairs and the major events that had occurred in my life.

What became clear from our conversation is that I was doing almost nothing for myself. I had become so oriented to the demands of others, as well as those of my own inner taskmaster, that I had no room left for anything else. About the only simple pleasure I allowed myself was playing my guitar now and then. As she succinctly put it, "Craig, you've been sweeping the dirt under the carpet for the last ten years, and now you just tripped over it." In closing the session, she recommended that I begin doing whatever I could to nurture myself—going out with a friend, joining a band (I am a fairly decent guitarist), and so on—to get through this difficult time.

Driving home from her office, I thought back to my meditation practice of many years ago and how effective it had been in improving my experience of everyday life. I quickly resolved that resuming this practice would be my treat to myself. Somehow, in spite of all the pressing demands on my time, I would make room for two twenty-minute meditation periods. In short order, I prepared a space with a special chair in the guest bedroom that I could use to restart my practice for twenty minutes in the early morning and again when I got home from work.

For the next two months, I meditated consistently, twice each day. It wasn't long before I reached the same plateau as I had in my earlier experience. I began to feel more relaxed and detached from my emotions, although the longing was still there. I started wondering why I couldn't go deeper into myself, so to speak, especially since my level of commitment and my ability to get centered even on bad days, were more evident than before. Each day's meditations were more or less the same in terms of the level of peacefulness I felt.

**Sudden Expansion**

Then, on the morning of Mother's Day 1999 I sat for my usual meditation and proceeded to consciously relax my body and clear my mind. Only this time, for reasons unknown to me, I had a much greater degree of focus and concentration than ever before. This is very difficult to convey in words, but after a certain point I felt my awareness suddenly expand so that I experienced myself as being infinite. The only way I can express this feeling is that I was within an endless void, and I was everywhere at once inside it, and yet, I still continued to maintain a sense of identity specific to myself. I had no sense of time or space; it seemed as if I was in another dimension, that my body was no longer there. Along with this was the experience of profound bliss and peace that permeated every part of me. I had attained a state of well-being that I never had remotely reached in my life, yet somehow it was not unfamiliar to me. Later, looking back, I realized that the ineffable essence of all things alluded to in the ancient Hindu statement "Thou Art That" was what I had felt. In that moment, I intuited, indeed, I Am That.

> The ineffable essence of all things alluded to in the ancient Hindu statement "Thou Art That" was what I had felt. In that moment I intuited, indeed, I Am That.

After a while, I sensed that it was time to return to the world, so I slowly opened my eyes and stretched. I looked at the clock and realized that over an hour had elapsed. For the remainder of the day, the peace and bliss stayed with me. I felt as if I was vibrating at a cellular level and that my body was lighter, not necessarily in weight, but in density. Paradoxically, I appeared to be saturated with a new energy that was substantial, almost to the point of being material. After this event, I settled into a pattern where my meditations were longer, and I seemed to approach, but not quite reach, this state of bliss about once per week. During these periods, I felt very little chance of experiencing any negativity because of what was happening around me.

Naturally, it wasn't long before I was asking myself what power I had tapped into. I knew no one around me would be able to relate to this, so I went to the bookstore to find out more. Looking through the sections on religion and New Age (I have grown to dislike the tired cliché this term has become) philosophy, I found books on dozens of different windows into the house of spirituality. Eventually, I settled on a book about astral projection, a form of out-of-body experience, or OBE. This book, *Astral Projection for Beginners* by Edain McCoy, ignited an intense interest in finding out if I could have some of these experiences.

In retrospect, I think my motivation at this stage was twofold. One purpose was to create excitement through these mysterious pursuits that would satisfy my longing. It was exhilarating to think that fantastic mystical adventures were actually possible and that maybe they could provide me a way to rise above the mundane world of problems everyone else faced. The other purpose was to use whatever I was tapping into to resolve the long-standing anxiety I had diminished in therapy, but had never completely conquered. It occurred to me that perhaps I was directly accessing my subconscious and that I could somehow fix my imperfections at the level of their root cause, all without having to understand how it actually happened. But, I am certain that I had no intent yet to accelerate spiritual growth or become enlightened. I do remember reading about the progression one could take through expanding consciousness and the resulting spiritual knowledge that would accrue; but, at the time, I wasn't interested in this path.

So, I redoubled my efforts and, to my surprise and satisfaction, I began to have additional mystical adventures along with the blissful experiences. While I didn't have any typical OBEs, as McCoy's book described, where a person looks back to see the material body lying motionless as he or she moves into the astral realm, I did have one very meaningful out-of-body experience. One thing this book, and many of the other books I have subsequently read, describes is that each of us is continually in the company of spirit guides who are always available to assist us. Most of us have heard the term *guardian angel,* and, indeed, I have learned that nonphysical entities are present, ready to help us traverse the path to awakening.

One day as I was meditating, when I reached a deep state of relaxation, I decided to summon my guide to present him/herself to me. After a few minutes without a response, I concentrated as hard as I could, almost pleading for my guide to show up.

Suddenly, the benignly smiling face of a man appeared in my mind; the man's name, I was told, was Edgar. This was told to me not by audible words, but by an internal form of communication that I can only describe as a direct sharing of thoughts. I was startled that this was actually happening, and the faint desire to reconsider all of what I had set in motion began to creep into my consciousness. Then, in an instant, I had left my physical body still sitting in my chair in the guest bedroom. I found myself in the master bathroom looking into the mirror, my face looking back at me. When I say I found myself in the bathroom, I mean my conscious awareness was there. The *me* that was really *me* was no longer attached to my body and could move anywhere at the speed of thought, sensing the surroundings wherever it happened to be. In the next instant, I (again, my conscious awareness) was flying across our backyard and the fields beyond, suddenly stopping outside the house where I had lived when I was thirteen, at the time of my father's death.

Somehow, I was revisiting the day of his death—again, the day before my bar mitzvah—with a specific focus on what was going through my mind at that time. I was being flooded with memories of the thoughts I had had then about inviting virtually my entire class to my big event, even though I wasn't really friendly with most of them. I was the type of kid who had a few best friends, but was not wildly popular or a member of the "in" crowd at my junior high school. Most specifically, I remembered having the feeling of shame that I was inviting a lot of kids I wasn't close to just to fill out the slate so I could appear cool and socially acceptable.

The amazing things about this recollection are, first, that I don't ever remember having thought about this episode since my father's passing. Second, when I suddenly remembered this thought thirty years later, it was as if I had never forgotten it. Third, and most obvious, is the fact that this thought must have been very significant to me if it was suddenly surfacing so dramatically after all this time, although I didn't know exactly why. What was Edgar trying to show me? Thinking back, perhaps he was helping me to see that I never had anything to be ashamed of and that it was finally time to release this unnecessary and shadowy burden.

All at once, I was back in my physical body, but still in a deeply relaxed state. Edgar appeared again, and I felt strange sensations in my gut, as if things were being rearranged. Edgar said "trust me" so I took his advice and continued to relax as this rearrangement continued for a few moments more. Of course, I didn't know exactly what was being moved around, or why, and I am not suggesting that anything had physically swapped places. However, the human body has much more to it than can be objectively observed, including many nonphysical structures and energy gradients.*

From that point forward, I felt differently in many situations involving negativity or strong ego feelings. Whenever I would find myself moving into an ego place, whether being self-aggrandizing, dishonest, or so on, I would feel strong discomfort in my solar plexus and the pit of my stomach. I also experienced a strong aversion to confrontation and feelings of anger. What's more, upon giving my nonjudgmental attention to these ego feelings, they would often transmute into ones of peace and contentment.† These feelings have waxed and waned over time, but they are always there.

I honestly don't know why this nonphysical entity was called Edgar or why he materialized at just that moment. Never having known anyone on earth by that name, and never having been exceedingly moved by any historical Edgars, Poe or Cayce, for instance, I gathered that the event itself at that stage in my life was important. As I have watched similar transformational episodes occur over a period of years, the mystery of the form they take and

---

\* One example appears in Chapter 3, An Unexpected Detour, in the discussion of kundalini.

† This powerful practice is discussed at length in Eckhart Tolle's book *The Power of Now;* see review in Chapter 9.

their timing fascinates me. Why then, and why that particular experience? What lesson was I to uncover? It seems that we really are much more than we believe ourselves to be, and that larger parts of ourselves really are available to help make this evident to us should we choose to open up to this possibility.

## A Promising Potential

Shortly after this episode, it began to slowly occur to me that the longing and all of these changes in my life were really about spiritual growth. Again, when I use the word *spiritual,* I don't consider it to pertain to religion or morality, as so many people do. It was becoming clearer to me that being spiritual meant waking up to, and directly experiencing, Reality in all of its fullness and splendor. I was beginning to realize that spiritual growth transcends religious concepts and what we accept culturally as right and wrong. I actually would be required to unlearn much of what I had unquestioningly taken to be the truth over the years. The direct experiences of Reality I was having were going to make this unavoidable.

I began to read books with different spiritual and scientific points of view, and I started to pay attention to my dreams, keeping a journal of them whenever possible. Many modern sources, beginning with Carl Jung most prominently, say dreams convey much more than we suspect. Carlos Casteneda and Seth, channeled through Jane Roberts, go a step further in saying that the dream state is as real as our normal waking awareness and that we can examine it consciously.* Apparently, in the dream state with its amorphous forms, the key is to first achieve repeated focus on very discrete objects, while in the more tangible waking state, to become aware of the whole is one of the basic paths to higher consciousness.† In any case, it seemed that I had much to

---

\* See their books, *The Art of Dreaming* and *The Nature of Personal Reality,* reviewed in Chapter 9.

† Paying attention to the present moment, or practicing mindful-ness, will lead to more awareness of everything at once, otherwise

explore within a significant part of my life I had been taking for granted.

I noticed a theme of increasing self-worth running through some of my dreams. Many of them contained people from my past in which I was in a state of having all of my personal power available to me, not a controlling power, but one of self-assurance and security. These dreams were in contrast to the way it had actually been in the past when I was in the habit of relinquishing my power to others. Another type of dream seemed to suggest that my life would be changing and that I would be going in an unspecified new direction. The need to make the appropriate changes so that the "new" could come in and growth could continue was the apparent message. Making the changes these dreams seemed to be calling for has been an area of struggle for me, as I will discuss later.

Along with the dreams, two experiences occurred during my meditations that also indicated a spiritual purpose to what was unfolding. One day, while in a deep meditation, I suddenly had a very compelling vision of an outstretched hand holding a tin cup, while at the same time I distinctly heard (actually felt) the words "Don't be afraid to give." It wasn't clear to me if I should take the vision literally in terms of material giving or if its message was more general in the sense of giving love to those around me. But, I had no doubt of its intent to get my attention, or that the message was meant directly for me. This could have been a reinforcement of a universal principle of abundance that had recently come into my awareness: the act of giving away the thing you desire is a highly effective way to physically manifest more of the very same thing.* In any case, this reminder has stayed

---

known as the whole. At the other end of the spectrum are the concentration methods of meditation, which involve focusing on a particular object or thought (i.e., a mantra) to the exclusion of all other stimuli.

* See the channeling in Appendix A, which addresses at length the universal principles of manifesting abundance.

with me over the years as a point of reference in widely diverse situations where I must make a decision about giving in its many forms.

The second episode was a very powerful one happening a short time later, once again while I was meditating. I was still trying to conjure up an out-of-body experience and was having no success. After spending some time attempting this in my highly relaxed state I gave up and impulsively started to pray to God. I don't remember the specifics of my prayer, but the instant I turned my attention to God, an energy of incredible love began emanating outward from my heart area. This outpouring continued for what must have been several minutes. The best I can do is to say that the presence of the Divine was within me at that instant, and of this fact, I have absolutely no doubt. No earthly counterpart that I know of exists to the feeling of oceanic peace and comfort I encountered in those moments. It may help to visualize this force as Life itself flowing in shimmering, ever-expanding waves from its Divine Source located in my heart. I knew then that I was not alone and that my existence had purpose, even though it was well beyond my ability to articulate it by any conventional means. So powerful was this experience that it took some time for me to even acknowledge, let alone assimilate, the magnitude of what had happened. Many

> I knew then that I was not alone and that there was purpose to my existence, even though it was well beyond my ability to articulate it by conventional means.

times, when I face uncertainty, or I struggle with the conflicts that arise between simultaneously living in both the spiritual and physical worlds, I think about this encounter with Divine Love to comfort me.

During that summer, as I continued my meditations, I seemed to go deeper and deeper. It was getting to the point where I was feeling a profound energy and power surging through me all day long. It felt as if my body was vibrating and that, at certain times, I could just float away. At work, I knew my colleagues noticed changes in me, as I stopped participating in the same conversation loops I always had before; those usually involved with gossip and complaint. I also spoke up in meetings with a forcefulness I did not previously possess. I was not being hostile, but I was now exhibiting a lesser concern for other's opinions of me, a new detachment that I truly felt. At home, my family was having a hard time with my changing behavior. The responses I used to give, even during arguments, were no longer there, and they sometimes felt as if they didn't recognize me anymore. But, I persisted in my new practice; I was like a moth to a flame. I wanted more energy and more power. While I was beginning to understand the spiritual nature of what I had undertaken, I didn't yet understand the consequences of being impatient or of doing what I was doing for just for the excitement of it.

Around this time, I had what I thought was another very meaningful dream. I was in a hospital at one end of a long hallway. People were sitting all along the length of the hallway as far as I could see. I started moving, slowly at first, to get to other end. While I was moving slowly, the people around me were normal and healthy, but still I felt compelled to go faster to get to the other end more quickly. As I picked up speed, the people began to look less healthy, and the faster I went, the more grotesque the people became. Eventually, it reached the point where they were missing body parts and were in advanced stages of decay. Then, I woke up. The next day, upon reflecting on this dream, I knew my message was to slow down. Of course, I didn't do so, and it led to some intensely uncomfortable experiences, but ones that turned out to be timely and appropriate for me.

# Chapter 3

## An Unexpected Detour

> When the world seems to be falling apart, the
> rule is to hang onto your own bliss. It's that life
> that survives.      —*Joseph Campbell*

> We do not know where our spiritual life will lead
> us, but it always requires us to go into that which
> is difficult and unknown.      —*Jack Kornfield*

Toward the end of the summer of 1999, I was surfing the Internet one day and decided to do a search on the word *kundalini*, a term I encountered in a book that mentioned it in passing as being associated with increased sexual energy. Being ever the intrepid explorer, I found a fairly comprehensive Web site that defined this term and then conveyed a lot more information that I found shocking and deeply disturbing.

According to this site, and subsequent books I have consulted on this subject, kundalini is the universal spiritual energy that animates us as we live our lives on earth. Normally, it resides in a nonphysical structure (or, at least one that science cannot currently detect) of the Human body near the base of the spine and is released slowly over the course of one's lifetime. When it is released, in a normal scenario, it flows upward to the crown of the head and beyond by way of three nonphysical channels, or

25

nadis (the Sushumna, Ida, and Pingala), traversing the seven main energy centers, or chakras, of the body.

Knowledge of kundalini energy, known as Shakti, the "divine spark of life," moving through the body, and the Chakras emanated from India thousands of years ago. Today, kundalini yoga* is better known as the discipline whose purpose is to work with this energy to experience cosmic consciousness in a spiritually beneficial fashion. Some think that the Caduceus—the two snakes intertwined around a central pillar that symbolizes the medical profession—was actually an ancient representation of kundalini energy flowing up the nadis. In fact, kundalini has also been referred to as the "serpent energy." The Chinese have a similar system of ancient knowledge that refers to a person's spiritual energy within the body as Chi. Chi energy follows meridians or pathways around the body, invigorating it, and helping a person attain higher states of spiritual awareness.†

However, in some situations people have experienced the release of this spiritual energy virtually all at once. On

---

\*   According to Dr. Stanislav Grof in *The Cosmic Game* (6), "the yogis see kundalini as the creative energy of the universe that is feminine in nature. It lies dormant in the sacral area of the human subtle body until it is activated by a guru, by meditation practice, or by some other influences. The close connection that exists between this spiritual energy and the sexual drive plays an essential role in kundalini yoga and in Tantric practices."

†   Although these ancient Indian and Chinese systems contain perhaps the most advanced body of knowledge available concerning this life force (aside from the systems of various indigenous societies), it is a natural rather than a religious or cultural phenomenon and is common to all human beings. It may be that paranormal states within other religious systems (e.g., talking in tongues) are actually manifestations of the awakening of this same universal energy.

the Web site there were many firsthand accounts from people that had undergone a full kundalini awakening. According to this information, these awakenings were triggered by various experiences of a highly intense nature, including childbirth, back trauma, and last but not least, very deep meditation. The results included everything from heightened spiritual awareness and psychic abilities, to powerful bursts of energy manifesting in manic behavior, to periods of deep depression and unexplainable physiological distress.

An awakening where the energy travels unimpeded up through the chakras leads to the structures of the persona literally being consumed, leaving an individual with a clean karmic slate, although someone who is completely changed. But, if fear or unresolved ego dynamics at a particular chakra block the energy, the result could be months or even years of psychological misery. It is even possible for damage to bodily tissues and organs to occur when they are subjected to the localized buildup of this energy.

The most widely referenced case of a traumatic kundalini awakening in the sources I checked was a first-person account from India documented in the book, *Living with Kundalini*, by Gopi Krishna. In Mr. Krishna's case, the energy did not move cleanly up through the nadis; years of suffering elapsed before he was able to clear it. I have subsequently read about others in our culture that had no idea what had happened to them, having never heard about kundalini. The psychiatric profession has not historically recognized spiritual energy as a valid determinant of a person's state of mind, its predisposition having been to label someone as psychotic instead.[*]

Imagine my reaction when I read about these stories. Here I was, feeling the awakening of tremendous energy within me during a relatively short period of time, one that I was sensing palpably every day throughout my body. Now I was confronting

---

[*]  See Spiritual Emergency in Chapter 8 for more information.

the possibility that, due to my intense meditation, I may have inadvertently brought myself to the brink of some cataclysmic event, where I would either lose my personality or spend years wandering in a psychological wilderness. Either way, it seemed that, very soon, I would no longer be the same person; indeed, I may not even be able to function as I always had in the world. I was finally internalizing the fact that

> I was finally internalizing the fact that radical transformation came with the territory on the quest I had begun.

radical transformation came with the territory on the quest I had begun and that had been gaining momentum for months. Did I want to change, I mean, really change? Could I stop the train and get off now? What would happen to me if I could not?

That evening, a Thursday, as I recall, I was tossing a baseball with my younger son in the backyard. During our catch, inexplicably, I began to have very strange, new feelings, so I told my son that I had to stop. Again, this ordeal is very difficult to portray in words, but it felt as if the edges of something dark and foreboding were coming toward me. My legs felt rubbery, and my breath was short. I went into the living room, lay down on the sofa, and closed my eyes. My head began to spin, and I experienced my consciousness moving away from my body; but, for some reason, I sensed that this time, it would not be temporary. I became frightened and opened my eyes, hoping it would stop. But I didn't seem to be returning to normal, and I couldn't shake these sensations.

At this point, I got up, walked into the kitchen, leaned on the countertop, and held onto it for dear life. Thankfully, no one else was in the house. The fright that I was feeling was now turning into terror, and it kept building. Ultimately, I reached a place where I actually felt myself standing on the edge of an abyss, endless and awful; I feared that if this process did not stop, my mind would be ripped apart. I was literally consumed with panic having not the slightest idea where this energy was taking me or what would happen to me when I got there. My entire internal sense of self and the taboos and inhibitions that inherently define a person's place in the world were about to be destroyed. As heavenly as my experiences of Spirit were before, such was the degree of hell I now saw in front of me. I found myself pleading to God to pull me back and to let my life remain as it was. Believe me when I say that I am not overdramatizing any of this, and that I am trying to be as true to my experience as I can.

Then, the terror finally subsided. I noticed that I hadn't gone beyond the edge of the abyss. Still, I was extremely agitated over what had just happened. I felt a strong need to immediately separate myself from what I realized I didn't remotely understand. So, I went to the guest bedroom, grabbed my meditation chair, and threw it in the trash. The books on astral projection went into the trash, as well. That night, I got very little sleep as energy akin to electricity ran through my body every hour or so. My thoughts centered on being vigilant in case the terror returned and wondering whether I could make it through work the next day. Although I felt extremely uncomfortable through the weekend, with recurring instances of energy bursts and uncertainty, by the following week, my state of being returned to the one with which I was familiar.

Now I was left with trying to sort things out. First, I resolved to cease meditating for the foreseeable future. (As an aside, about two weeks later, I sat down to start meditating just to see what would happen. As soon as I closed my eyes, I began to be swept away again. I stopped immediately.) Second, at a very basic level, I knew that the journey I had embarked on was truly spiritual, and that the enhanced personal power I was seeking had a much different meaning than I had been ascribing to it. Moreover, I realized the journey was one that I needed to take more time to absorb. However, I was certainly not going to forsake this process. I now had internal experiential proof that the Divine was real and, whatever the twists and turns my path would take, I just couldn't deny it.

## Getting Grounded

I remembered a point someone had made in one of the accounts on the kundalini Web site that suddenly seemed very appropriate for me. After having some overwhelming Divine encounters, this person saw that, for the time being, the way to mastery was by practicing love and the release of negativity in everyday, mundane situations with those with whom we are usually in contact. This was perhaps a more prosaic aspect of spiritual growth, but I knew I had been missing it. To validate this supposition, and to help me understand the

> Recognize and work with thoughts and words, accepting responsibility for the mind's contents and, by extension, whatever manifests as a result.

nature of my experiences, I accelerated my exploration of spiritual and scientific information.

Indeed, a fundamental theme raised by virtually every source of true spiritual wisdom I have since seen is the power our thoughts and words have in shaping our experience of reality. One's thoughts and words are literally energy, and combined with sincere intent, they cause the Universe to bring a person exactly what this energy calls forth. A mind continually fixated on thoughts of fear, anger, worry, guilt, and the like, will attract events in kind. The challenge is to recognize and work with thoughts and words, accepting responsibility for the mind's contents and, by extension, whatever manifests as a result. If one accepts this premise (as I do), it isn't hard to see that progressively changing the everyday use of the mind to one based on love is helpful for experiencing the power of the Divine in a loving way.

It occurred to me that, even with nine years of psychological counseling, I had really paid very little attention in real time to the contents of my mind. I decided to practice observing the mental chatter to assess its quality. It might seem that watching one's thoughts for any length of time might drive a person crazy, and, shortly, I began to appreciate the descriptions I had seen of the mind as a "drunken monkey" or a cork bobbing along on a raging river. However, while I could only observe the chatter for brief periods, with relatively long spaces in between them, I found that I soon could identify and at least slow down the negative, ego-based tape loops that consumed so much of my thinking. The key was to try to observe my thoughts without judgment and without imposing on myself the requirement to do anything about them. The practice of *just giving attention whenever possible to the present moment* seemed to help me.

But, once more, my longing for adventure, in the guise of spiritual research, got the better of me. One of the sources I wanted to consult in my quest for greater understanding was *Living with Kundalini*, the book I mentioned earlier. About a month after my near meltdown, I ordered this book from Amazon.com. On numerous prior occasions when I had ordered anything from Amazon, I never had a problem with delivery of the goods to my home. So, it was very interesting that a few days after ordering this book, Hurricane Floyd roared up the East Coast, and the book never materialized. Of course, I later realized that this was a synchronicity, a message telling me to leave well enough alone. Not seeing this at the time, I called Amazon, and they promptly shipped another copy to me.

On a Friday evening after finally receiving the book, I sat down and read just the first chapter. Gopi Krishna, the author, related the onset of his kundalini awakening, what a shock it was to him, and how his life started to completely unravel. Then a strange thing happened. The moment I put the book down, with no warning, I began to feel the same terror from a month before coming toward me. Again, I went down to the kitchen (everyone else was upstairs) and proceeded to go through much the same events as I had the first time. Although the terror was less intense than it had been before, it was very strong. Again, I begged God to pull me back.

Eventually, it faded, and I spent the night with waves of electric-like energy flowing through me. Only this time, for some reason, I did not fear it, and it felt wonderful, as if I were made of "liquid love," a term Gopi Krishna used. The next day, Saturday, I was completely out of sorts because my usual sense of self was not totally available to me. Nevertheless, I kept an appointment with some friends to help them purchase and install window shades in their house. Focusing on this all-day job helped me endure the weekend, and again, I returned to feeling normal early the following week. But that book remained on my shelf unread, and for quite a while, kundalini became somewhat of bogeyman for me.

# Chapter 4

## On the Road Again

*The way to succeed is to keep one's courage and patience, and to work on energetically.*
—*Vincent Van Gogh*

After about six months, I gingerly started to meditate again. Within several more months, I was back to a daily practice, which I have continued to the present day. My experiences over the past several years have included a variety of wonderful encounters with nonphysical Reality, some during meditation, some while awake in everyday situations, and some while sleeping during the dream state. But, these encounters have been less frequent than before, and this period can be characterized as somewhat quieter. Sometimes there have been stretches during which nothing much seems to be happening. I am at peace

> Sometimes, spiritual growth is plain, old-fashioned hard work, but it is well worth it considering that the alternative is continuing to exist in a state of unconsciousness.

with this having come to learn that a primary feature of spiritual growth is rest and consolidation of prior experience. Nothing is forgotten.

I also maintained my exploration of published material. Another book with a different slant, yet one consistent with the image of the Universe as loving and life affirming, always seemed to present itself to me at just the right time. The messages were always the same: release your fear, stay in the present, and take responsibility for the reality you find yourself experiencing. Make a daily practice of releasing deep-rooted ego habits that are grounded in fear. Sometimes, spiritual growth is plain, old-fashioned hard work, but it is well worth it to me when I remember that the alternative is continuing to exist in a state of unconsciousness.

I believe I have given up my dread of kundalini, now realizing that these episodes were a gift given to me so that I could appropriately absorb the underlying lesson about the importance of releasing fear. I even wonder whether I was on the verge of a kundalini awakening. It's possible that I was about to undergo a fundamental, permanent shift in consciousness, what many would call enlightenment. Either way, I trust that the next time a moment of transformation presents itself, I will not turn away in fear. I also know that my role is not to dictate the timing of my awakening, but to allow it to happen when it does come.

To some degree, I have struggled with the issue of whether I should make external changes in my life to accommodate greater awareness of Reality. One recurring principle in the process of spiritual growth is that letting go of the old is necessary to make way for the new, just as the clearing of dead brush is needed before new vegetation can grow. The old could be where a person lives, a relationship, certain material possessions, a vocation, cherished beliefs, or anything to which one has become attached and that no longer serves the evolution of the soul. Change, especially when it is motivated by inner shifts that others cannot see, is a hard thing to face; but, it is nonetheless inevitable. I often see others I know going through painful upheaval in their lives, and I secretly admire them for being willing, even if they may not be aware of it, to do what they must do to move forward.

After giving this considerable thought, I have decided to let the changes come to me instead of purposefully initiating them.

Early on, my inclination was to believe that drastic alteration of my life was a requirement for further growth. Perhaps I should quit my job and work in a food bank or travel to the spiritual centers of India or Mexico. My understanding has gradually come to be that the expansion of one's consciousness occurs right where he or she happens to be, and everything necessary to this process will unfold from there. I have chosen to maintain what Eckhart Tolle (29) calls

> The expansion of consciousness occurs right where one happens to be, and everything necessary to this process will unfold from there.

one's life situation, which for me, I can currently characterize as suburban-Jewish-American-professional-family-man-in-the-early-twenty-first-century. My job now is to recognize the changes as they materialize and have the courage to accept them, whether it means letting in new adventures or letting go of what no longer has purpose for me, even if the ultimate result is a fundamental alteration in my life situation.

## Being Anew

One new direction I have already accepted is to move beyond the limits of a particular religion's beliefs and not feel inhibited to incorporate whatever resonates with my internal knowing, regardless of the source. Although I feel the truth of the messages in some of my inherited religion's prayers and beliefs, I now find others to be limited and misguided, artifacts of a world we are leaving behind. A god who judges, has conditions, or requires praise, or a prayer that asks for blessing for only a certain people or land, doesn't square with me anymore. During a religious observance, when I feel the need, I either remain silent or change the words of the prayers to suit myself.

At the same time, I am surprised to find that I now can enjoy certain aspects of my outwardly traditional Jewish-American lifestyle to a degree not possible before. As far as Judaism is concerned, the biggest surprise to me is that, when I do attend services at the synagogue now, I get more out of them on an experiential level than at any time in the past. My sons' recent bar mitzvahs, in particular, were two of the most joyous events of my life, almost as joyous as seeing both of them being born. At one point during my younger son's service, the cantor sang the old Bob Dylan song, "Forever Young," accompanying himself on his guitar. All at once, I felt the entire spectrum of emotions a father feels for his son—all of my hopes and dreams for him, and the sudden clarity of seeing his life forever intertwined with mine. I wept softly at this understanding, right there in front of over one hundred people, and thought how much more meaningful it was to me than anything in the prayer book.

And, paradoxically, as I have become less beholden to religious beliefs, I have noticed an emerging reverence for the beauty in many of the trappings of Judaism: the haunting melody of the Haftarah,* the mystery of the ancient Hebrew letters, the familiar cycle of holidays as the years pass. The pithiness of Yiddish, the sensation of Jewish soul food, and the irreverence of Jewish humor all imbue my experience. At a higher level, Jewishness is an inescapable part of my character in this life, part of the props on my stage, as it were, independent of any of the beliefs I choose to hold.

On the secular side of my life, many blessings have also materialized. Among them, believe it or not, is a strong affinity for the game of golf. It was actually my younger son who caught the golf bug first at age eleven while playing a video game featuring Tiger Woods. Suddenly, I was schlepping him to the local chip and putt, and then to regulation courses, almost every other weekend. It didn't take long before I realized that I was being seduced by the nuances of the game, the idyllic surroundings, and the wonderful times my son and I were sharing together.

---

\* The Haftarah, a portion taken from one of the books of Prophets (such as Isaiah and Jeremiah), became part of the Shabbat service about nineteen hundred years ago when the Roman Empire outlawed the reading of the Torah in public.

But, beyond that, I have noticed how ironic it is that golf, the paragon of old-world, high-society leisure, is also the perfect Zen practice. As anyone who has chased the little white ball can attest, the more frustrated you become and the more willful you are, the worse you do. Fulfillment can only be found in the present shot; fuming over your last shot or worrying about what your score will be only leads to suffering. So, aside from aspiring to enlightenment, I am also attempting to grow spiritually to break a score of one hundred. *

With my older son, I have discovered the simple pleasure of long bike excursions, sometimes thirty miles or more, through some gorgeous countryside and area parkland. He is also becoming an accomplished guitarist and my built-in jamming partner right down the hall. As I reflect on what I have just described, it occurs to me that, while I may have sometimes thought their worldly needs conflicted with my spiritual practice, my family has actually helped me to find the joy in life, an essential element of spiritual growth for anyone.

One area of daily living that I have honestly found quite puzzling is work. Earlier I mentioned how I had been promoted to a director-level position soon after my awakening began; I inferred that this was somewhat of a breakthrough for me. Soon after that moment, however, any semblance of career progress vanished as the company, along with the marketplace, fell on lean times, mainly because of the great dot.com implosion in 2001. Recent years have been filled with wrenching dislocations, like watching people lose their jobs and being jarred by continually

---

\* A while after writing these words, I was surprised to find an eminent spiritual teacher and a Zen master each mentioned in Jack Kornfield's book, *After the Ecstatsy, the Laundry*, who expressed a desire to find more time to play golf. At first, I was somewhat disconcerted by the thought of highly evolved beings sporting regulation golf attire (or do they stay in their saffron robes?), but perhaps the concept of golf as a sanctioned spiritual practice is one whose time has come.

shifting objectives and cost reductions, including pared back compensation and benefits.

Lately, the reasons for all of the upheaval have resolved into sharper focus for me. One prospect is the role I may play in helping balance the tone of my uneasy work environment. After realizing that I had been walking around for years with a clenched jaw and my antennae always alert for incoming missiles, I decided that that it was not at all mandated that I must be miserable in order to be competent. As I experience more inner calm and my behavior changes accordingly, perhaps in subtle ways, the influence of my demeanor is moving the collective consciousness of the company to a healthier state. Although I imagine that some of my co-workers would have a good guffaw at this suggestion, I try to remember that we continually influence each other in many ways, seen and unseen, and to look for evidence of this principle whenever possible.

> It is not at all mandated that one must be miserable in order to be competent.

Working conditions have also put the issue of abundance, or really trust, squarely in my path. The cost of raising my family and maintaining our lifestyle has gone up as my kids have matured, even as my compensation has been curtailed. I now see that I am being asked to use my intent more than ever to let my full abundance in, trusting that Spirit will manifest it completely and tangibly, regardless of appearances that seem to argue to the contrary. I accept as a universal truth my inherent power and free will to create any reality I choose. But, the question I am actually being asked to wrestle with is whether I will now trust enough to make it true in my experience.*

---

* Although economic uncertainty continued to remain a fact of life in our business environment, sure enough, conditions eventually improved. I received another promotion and an increase in pay that brought me to the level I would have attained had no dot.com collapse occurred.

At deeper levels, certain aspects of my persona have changed, as well. For one thing, I have noticed a difference in my sense of humor. In the past, many considered me a funny person, but frankly, my humor was often a cutting one that came at the expense of others' deficiencies or misfortunes. I don't think it's a stretch to say that my humor arose from my own considerable anxieties. Today, with fewer defenses to maintain, I find that my humor is now suffused with much more joy and unabashed loonyness than before. With my sons, especially, I have delighted in taking the opportunity to express myself in a more childlike (some would say juvenile) way around them whenever possible. Lately, of course, I have had to be careful to respect their teenage sensibilities, which dictate that it's a disaster for Dad to act like a lunatic in public and an unforgivable extinction-level-event to do so around their friends.

Related to this change is the discovery of a new dimension in the experience of the arts, especially music. When I was a child, the grandeur of *Tchaikovsky's Piano Concerto No. 1* evoked in me a sense of poignancy and romance, inspiring my twelve-year-old imagination. After exploring and relishing virtually the entire spectrum of musical expression in the decades that followed, I have found myself returning again and again to the great classical works. It's not just the mystery of how a creation so exquisitely elaborate and magnificent came to be. My old sentimentality seems to have been greatly amplified, as well. Listening to this same masterpiece now, I hear a deep compassion for humanity, in spite of all its blemishes, and a remarkable jubilance as the music's denouement portends our collective transcendence of the suffering we inflict on ourselves. Many sources say that true art, in whatever form, is by its nature divinely inspired. Joseph Campbell (33), the eminent scholar of mythology and culture, referred to this idea as a sense of "esthetic arrest" induced by "divinely superfluous beauty."[3] Now, I know what he meant.*

As I alluded earlier, I stopped eating meat in 2000 after reading about how literally millions of animals are subjected to the most inhumane torture imaginable every day as part of the food industry's drive for lower costs and higher productivity.[4] Even though I had been a lifelong meat eater, it really wasn't as hard as one might think because, as my spiritual practice deepened, a burgeoning love of animals counterbalanced the withdrawal. The profound connection I feel to all of nature—the trees, the rain, my body—has become such that, at times, I am overcome by the astonishing miracle of it all.

The flip side of my powerful realization of the beauty and splendor of the planet is the equally powerful sorrow I often feel at what we humans are doing to destroy this paradise. It's crystal clear to me on a visceral level that our domination and exploitation of all other forms of life cannot continue. I now see that the human condition has arisen because, collectively, we have built a world of illusory structure on top of what is actually Real, and we have baked into our experience the illusion we have manufactured. Our structures are truly grand, be they impenetrable tax codes, trade laws, or insurance regulations; huge automobiles that require countless gallons of fossil fuel and acres of roads and parking lots to hold them; divisive, exclusionary, and

---

\* As an aside, it occurred to me that there is irony in the common notion of classical music as stuffy or elitist, as compared to the abandon of popular music, particularly jazz, blues, and rock and roll. If all true art is divinely inspired, and if divinity is characterized by unending Joy, then abandoning oneself to some of the most divine music ever written will reveal that this common notion is grossly mistaken. Of course, the culture of classical music sometimes contributes to this misconception by its overly serious and staid demeanor. Divine artistic expression and the experience of Joy are found in all types of music, regardless of the culture that surrounds them.

obdurate religious doctrines; or ingeniously effective techniques to better kill each other.

Societal institutions and technology are not the problem. Our collective intent that determines whether they truly serve us is the problem. The customary belief that we must use our natural endowment and conscious energy to build more impregnable defenses against malevolent forces that would upset our structures, has brought us to a world of unmanageable complexity and

> Once you remember what you have really always known, you will be filled with awe and wonder, as well as a familiarity that you can't explain.

imbalance. This imbalance is now becoming unsustainable, even at the level of the planet. We have been traveling down the path of the ego for many thousands of years, building upon and embellishing the same ideas about how the Universe operates and how to bend it to our will. But, it's now becoming obvious that these ideas no longer work. The ego is puny compared to the infinity of Nature; it can no longer manage the tools it has fashioned to bring Nature to heel, if such a thing were ever possible. We must soon rediscover the path of life-affirming wisdom we once traveled, but wandered away from, long ago.

Intriguing ideas to play with, but radical and scary to actually consider inviting into your life, don't you agree? Yes, but this is just the type of shift in perspective waiting for anyone who takes on the mantle of becoming a consciously aware human being. Enough individuals must be open to purposefully cultivating their own moments of illumination so that the "radical idealism of spirituality can be tangibly expressed in the world as the practical realism of healing."[5] As a critical mass of these willing souls is achieved, a release of outmoded, ancient beliefs can occur at last. When it does, the grand illusion we have manufactured will evaporate, leading to a collective and fundamental shift in human consciousness and a completely new way of living. The alternative is simply for us to allow this cycle of human experience on the earth to draw to a close.

As I stated before, it's anathema for most people I know to even consider these ideas, because they would lead to upheaval and change in their lives. But, for better or worse, I know in my heart that everyone, including me, will have to change, either by free will or force of circumstance. Accepting the necessary adjustments willingly while the opportunity still exists is certainly the more comfortable and wiser choice. As you might have guessed, I am optimistic that we humans will take the path of continuing evolution and expansion, and that we will soon be living in a world not based on power and control, but one that offers great empowerment and a vastly expanded experience of Reality for everyone.

# Chapter 5

## Walking the Talk

So other people hurt me? That's their problem.
Their character and actions are not mine. What
is done to me is ordained by nature, what I do by
my own.                              —*Marcus Aurelius*

For when I act in this worldcentric—not
egocentric, not ethnocentric, but worldcentric—
fashion, I am free in the deepest sense, for I am
obeying not an outside force but the interior force
of my own ethical reasoning; I am autonomous, I
am deeply free.                            —*Ken Wilber*

After my unsettling wake-up call, I opened up to a wide range of
inner experience that demanded the investment of my attention
and energy to explore further. As I have described, doing so was
not really a choice; I couldn't turn back, and it wasn't long before
I faced some monumental questions. How could I, as an ordinary
adult living a conventional twenty-first-century life, make sense
out of these encounters? They had no similarity to anything in
my everyday existence and no one around me would understand.
How could I possibly make room for this genie, now escaped
from the bottle, and cope with the changes to my familiar world

that were sure to come? What did it mean to "walk this talk" every day, while continuing to raise a family and earn a living?

I searched high and low for the insight to help decipher these riddles. The more I thought about how the wisdom I found correlated with my experience, the more it became apparent that I would be required to develop a new perspective on something I had always assumed I recognized—Love. I was now learning that true Love, in the larger Divine sense, is an absolutely tangible power that we can only know when we

> The repeated experience of Love in the larger Divine sense naturally leads one to act effortlessly in ways that the pious and righteous lay claim to, but don't often exhibit.

make the commitment to let go of fear, negativity, and self-importance in their many, everyday forms. I was seeing that being righteous or devout is not the true measure of spiritual maturity, but that simply allowing the feeling of Love to emerge is.

This seemed disconcerting at first, in light of prevailing beliefs, but it soon became obvious to me that embodying any of the traditional definitions of piety and being Loving are not equivalent. Righteousness, for instance, does not necessarily exemplify humility, gratitude, or forgiveness and, in fact, can be applied quite harshly. On the other hand, having the repeated experience of Love naturally leads one to act effortlessly in ways that the pious and righteous lay claim to, but don't often exhibit. Clearly, the characteristics of true Love were not what I had always assumed them to be.[*]

The same is also true in the larger sphere of the natural world beyond human interaction. This occurs to me now when I am walking my dog in the morning, and I am in a rush to get to work. In the middle of my impatience to attend to ostensibly

---

[*]   Let me note also that being Loving does not mean being constantly malleable, doing what everyone else wants. Its expression may sometimes require embracing difficult or lonely conditions that call for the courage to demand or initiate change.

respectable pursuits, I watch as she carefully inspects a shrub with her nose, and I remember that this natural function of hers is absolutely necessary to her vitality and fulfillment. By spending an extra few minutes on our walk, I am experiencing Love in a small but significant way. I am honoring my dog's desire to be what she divinely aspires to be, even if only for a short time. By willingly sharing that moment with her, I am freeing myself from the artificial burdens of irritation and stress.

I know this portrait of Love may seem counterintuitive at first, but allow for the moment that It is always there and eventually will make Itself known to each and every one of us in Its universal, less anthropomorphic form. Seemingly, out of nowhere, comes a wake-up call. A new and unfamiliar set of thoughts and feelings emerge that can be triggered by any number of agents, among them psychological upheaval (some form of mid-life crisis), disruptive life events (divorce or loss of employment), or unexpected expansion of awareness (unusually vivid dreams or transcendent experiences). While most people, up until this pivotal point, try to find the meaning of life through better understanding of their preexisting worldviews, new information or beliefs that suddenly seem inadequate may now motivate them to look beyond their old assumptions. In all of these cases, Love is knocking at our door, waiting to be let in.*

When Love comes knocking, we really have only two possible choices. Our more usual response is to not get up and open the door; that is, we continue to follow ingrained habits of thinking and repeat the same long-standing patterns of behavior. This is

---

* Three books give insightful personal accounts that portray the transformational nature of the spiritual search. Thom Hartmann's *The Prophet's Way* (30) tells the author's life story, while Caroline Myss's *Anatomy of the Spirit* (2) contains anecdotes of spiritual awakening from a variety of people in different life circumstances. *After the Ecstasy, the Laundry,* by Jack Kornfield (1), is a compassionate review of the highs, lows, and in-betweens of awakening supported by many historical and contemporary examples.

the familiar and seemingly stable, but quietly desperate, path of unconsciousness. The alternative, less common, response is to try being in a new way, mainly by listening within and allowing ourselves to be led in a direction that may induce change. This is the unseen and boundary stretching, but deeply fulfilling, path of awakening. It's essential to drop fear in its many forms to embrace this new path comfortably. Why? Because, at the bottom line, Divine Love becomes our guide on this path. Love is all there really is (see God is Love in Chapter 6), and awakening and surrendering to what is, essentially, the sum and substance of existence, can be daunting.

Developing trust in the inherent goodness of Love's unfolding is needed to increase the awareness of this fundamental energy of life in a balanced way. An analogy (40) makes this point quite clearly. You may be very relaxed being in a swimming pool with a depth of eight feet, thinking nothing of the amount of water surrounding you while you swim. But one day, you may go out in a fishing boat thirty miles from land and, because it's a warm, sunny day, decide to jump into the ocean and swim for a while. As you swim, it dawns on you that two-thousand feet of water now lie beneath you, stretching endlessly in every direction. Then fear enters your awareness. The process of swimming is the same in the ocean as it is in the pool, but without more trust, the sheer magnitude of the ocean can become overwhelming.

Divine Love is an ocean. Early on, when fear was present, I resisted the awareness of this energy. I eventually realized that steadily relinquishing fear, not only from ego dynamics, but also from the initial sense of being overwhelmed by the

> Love is woven into the fabric of each of our very beings and will find its way into our awareness at some point.

circumstances in which Love appears, is accomplished through patience and trust. As many people who begin to open their eyes, I have experienced this as what Jack Kornfield calls "a slow spiral, a steady and repetitive remaking of inner being [in which] the heart gradually deepens in knowing, compassion, and trust" (1). The new and unsettling circumstances in which you may find yourself are simply an invitation to look at the same old things in a different way. You embrace the discovery of Love over time in proportion to your willingness to let it emerge.

At the same time, we really have no way around this discovery. Individually, Love is woven into the fabric of each of our very beings and will, as stated earlier, find its way into our awareness at some point (see God Is All There Is of Us in Chapter 6). It is my sense that the same is true collectively. The accelerating turmoil we see around us on so many different fronts is evidence, not of the end of the world, but of a transformational shift in consciousness in which Love is materializing on a large scale. Because most of the world is still clinging to the old fear-based ways of being, this shift is hitting the fan, so to speak. The end of the world, as we know it, will not be ushered in by the appearance of a messiah who will save us. The transformation within ourselves will reveal that we never needed to be saved from anything. Heaven has been here all along. It's the experience that remains when we set aside all the artificial definitions we have given to everything (40). The only question is when we will decide to look inward to see what has never ceased to be.

**Opening to Love**

As this new meaning of Love beckoned to me through growing curiosity, the willingness naturally followed to explore it more fully in a purposeful way. I grasped that I was beginning a spiritual practice that would continue for the rest of my life and beyond, and would eventually cause my everyday world to reconfigure around me. Love would provide the new context for my unprecedented experiences. Love would give me the means to assimilate the inevitable changes in my life. Love would be the point of balance as I straddled two worlds, one inner and one outer. But, how was this shift actually going to happen?

The practice of meditation, as I have indicated, is the way I chose to open spiritually, although many other paths may lead Home. Over the years, I have had special moments while going within that gave me the keen insight that I was much more than I had previously imagined. The accumulation of these experiences formed the basis for knowing a truth that I cannot adequately communicate in words or enforce by commitment to a set of beliefs.

During one particular meditation, everything I considered as being part of my existence—the physical world and my identity in terms of job, family, country, and so forth—was suddenly reduced to a tiny yellow dot within an infinite field of blackness. I now observed the tiny dot from the perspective of this Void and realized that, as vast as what we can see and identify with seems to be, in reality, it is a miniscule part of who we really are, and the "much more" of ourselves possible for us to discover. I also understood that my tiny perspective wouldn't necessarily disappear, but its attraction for me in the grand scheme of the Void would become less significant by comparison.

In another instance, I experienced my body and personality as the topmost layer of a spiritual strata having unfathomable depth. It became apparent that underneath this superficial mask I present to the outside world exists the Divine Love I had begun to explore, in endless and ever subtler levels. I saw that the mask, such that it is, could not exist on its own without this ubiquitous Love. Not only that, but a fundamental characteristic of the Love was an intelligence beyond the dimensions of mind we usually recognize, compelling me to reach out to It and ask for Its guidance. In those moments, the answer was returned to me, not in words, but in deep feelings of exquisite peace and the instantaneous knowing that, as an integral, eternal, and irreplaceable part of the Whole, I was absolutely safe.

As I accumulated these and other insights, I found my heart softening while the crust of rigid beliefs, congealed over the centuries, began to disintegrate. Connectedness with the many levels of Being and with Nature became increasingly tangible. I started to view my physical world from an expanded perspective; yet, I also began to see disparities in stark relief between this new vantage point and the old one of the ego. Often these gaps were very difficult to reconcile, because the ego—my own and others—seemed to continually conspire to pull me back from my new understanding.

A primary question insinuated itself into the center of my attention: As my heart expanded, how could I coexist with the world I had known and in which I was still very much a willing participant? How could I function comfortably when, indeed, I felt more and more like a "stranger in a strange land"? I found myself wrestling with many and varied forms of this question in my life on a daily basis, including:

- How do I persuade someone who wants to swat a fly to instead let me open a window so it can be free rather than be killed? After all, what's the big deal? It's only a fly.
- How can I explain to my fellow Jews my understanding that all lands are sacred and all peoples of the world are chosen? After all, Israel is the ancient homeland of the Jewish people whose very survival is now at risk in exceedingly hostile surroundings.

> A primary question: How do I bring my spiritual understanding into existence in practical terms?

- What do I do at my son's school assembly as others recite the Pledge of Allegiance when I know that the entire world, not only one nation, will need to be indivisible under God? After all, these are childish, even dangerous, sentiments, especially when our country is facing the evil of terrorism worldwide.
- How do I deal with the quizzical expressions when I refuse plastic bags at the checkout or straws in restaurants, whenever possible, out of concern for the earth? After all, worrying about what ends up buried in the ground to

that extreme is ridiculous and everyone knows that one person's actions make no difference anyway.

- What can I say to someone in a position of influence who asks me to do something relatively minor, but unethical, when it has become repugnant for me to be dishonorable, or to dissemble and obfuscate? After all, everyone does it, no one will know, and it's the smart thing to do.

- How do I express my awe and reverence for geese, those majestic and highly familial birds, when everyone with whom I am eating lunch is complaining about how they are fouling up the parking lot? After all, isn't it true that too many of these pests are around nowadays? They poop everywhere and should be taken care of somehow.

- How do I satisfy someone's curiosity about why I meditate or no longer eat meat? After all, it's kind of interesting, but it's also quirky and weird behavior for a middle-aged, professional family man.

- How do I tell my sons that they are blessed with wealth beyond measure when they ask me whether we are rich? After all, they can't easily observe this spiritual truth, but they can clearly observe others who have much more materially than we do.

- How do I put into practice a paradoxical spiritual law such as: Getting more of something is best achieved by giving away some of the very same thing? After all, this idea seems to make absolutely no sense in a world that is obviously governed by the economic law of supply and demand.

- How will I continue allowing myself to let go of my best definitions of everything so that I may have more of the Truth revealed to me by Divine Intelligence? After all, the pleasure of using my rational mind, and applying it to achieve goals and solve problems, is as much a part of me as it was before my awakening.

So, how *do* I bring all of my spiritual understanding into existence in practical terms? The truth is, sometimes I don't. Often, I avoid doing what's in my heart when I believe others are not likely to receive it well. Sometimes, I do what I can around the edges of a particular situation, and at other times, I decide to go all the way, acting on my spiritual insight while throwing caution to the wind. In any event, I understand that transcending my fear, accumulated over a very long period of time, requires a long-term commitment to gradually complete the transformation that I have started and can no longer reverse.

## Adopting a Strategy for Spiritual Growth

Once my spiritual desire found expression in the world a few times, but with little context to give it perspective, I knew that adopting a strategy for spiritual growth would be essential. In time, through trial and error, and a lot of research, I realized that I had somewhat unwittingly incorporated such an approach into my life. I discovered I was pursuing three general areas of practice concurrently that have since complemented each other very well, helping me immeasurably as I continue to awaken in the world. These three practice areas, described here, would be beneficial for anyone with the desire to become a spiritual explorer in a meaningful, rewarding, and comfortable way.

- **Direct Experience**

Set aside a period of time each day to engage in a method of your choosing to become still, move beyond the limitations of the thinking mind, and have the genuine and immediate knowledge of your true Being. Meditation is one way, but many others work, too. The consistent practice of making direct contact with your inner Self eventually establishes within you an internal anchor point around which everything else ends up revolving. This new frame of reference gives you the courage to persist and to be patient with yourself as you take detours and try again. You will find a suggested meditation program, as well as an overview of other forms of practice, in the Experiential Guide in Chapter 7.

- **Waking Awareness**

Use normal events and encounters during your daily routine as opportunities to bring your direct experience into the world and enhance your life. During the periods between the illumination that direct experience can bring, your practice becomes one of consciously letting go of old fear-based habits and expressing Love in various ways. Countless situations in which you can do this will present themselves, as many as you can notice and take advantage of, but they all will help break down the ego barriers to personal transformation. Later in this chapter, practical ways are offered to release fear and to explore Love more fully every day.

- **Conceptual Understanding**

Explore the wisdom and teachings from various sources to promote understanding of direct experience and expanded awareness of Spirit. Review and contemplate published works to gain an understanding of what you have already experienced and to some extent, use them as a catalyst for further awakening. The Conceptual Guide in Chapter 9 addresses, at greater length, the nature of published spiritual and scientific works and cites many examples. I should also mention that group study or discussion might also have value for broadening your perspective, if you find this type of setting appealing. The most important thing to remember is that the value of concepts is to bring you to the point of experience. Don't become enamored with concepts as an end in themselves. They won't transform you; direct experience will.

These three fields of spiritual growth are related, as the simple diagram below illustrates.* The large, thin circle on the left shows the complete human being whose true nature is without

---

\*     This simple, yet very powerful conceptualization, is based on Raj's teachings (40).

limit in any way. The tiny circle in the center is the ego level of existence most of humanity usually chooses to operate within and, therefore, constrain itself to. Expanding the circle of the ego to the right reveals it to be nothing more than a boundary consisting of firmly held belief structures that reinforce a dualistic perception of reality. Spiritual awakening is the process of piercing this veil through Direct Experience. Practices of Waking Awareness (releasing fear and expressing Love in the world) and pursuit of Conceptual Understanding can help to facilitate the enlightenment that only Direct Experience can bring.

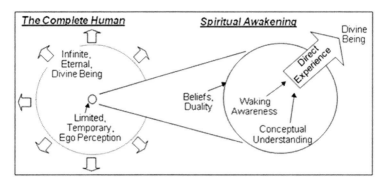

**Figure 1—The Human Being and Spiritual Awakening**

Being routinely active in these three areas of practice will eventually lead to self-empowerment and personal transformation. Many excellent books discuss the subject of spiritual growth and what to expect from various traditional and experiential viewpoints. My intent here is to describe some of the alternatives that have been most helpful to me. I encourage you to delve into the many available sources that explain their particular approaches and methods in detail.

Any practice, whether it concerns spiritual growth or playing the piano, needs regular expression. Just as you develop muscle memory in the fingers by repeatedly playing scales, you will gradually expand your awareness by giving your attention in various ways to spiritual growth on a daily basis. This doesn't mean you need to live in a monastery. But, if you decide to meditate for twenty minutes a day or to consciously bring more Joy into your life, for instance, stick with it. Give yourself a chance to open up to a new perspective.

The pursuit of directly finding inner peace and enlightenment has been with us for thousands of years, appearing in some form in virtually every culture and spiritual system, including the great religions. All of these practices are essentially about becoming still, going beyond thought into the silence within, and then being fully present and listening for whatever shows up (5,40). Using the example of

> Direct practice is all about becoming still, going beyond thought into the silence within, and then listening for whatever shows up.

meditation with which I am familiar,* various strategies exist to help disengage the mind from its usual incessant chattering. One is to concentrate on a word or phrase (i.e., a mantra) silently, or count numbers, giving as much attention as effortlessly as possible to the repetition. Another is to focus on the body's breathing cycle, which is always available and is completely natural and familiar. Still other methods are available, such as choiceless awareness, in which one completely defocuses attention to become aware of everything at once (the Whole), and guided meditations that employ spoken visualizations and affirmations, or music. In addition to the meditation program that I follow, presented in Chapter 7, other excellent methods of practice are given in *A Path With Heart* by Jack Kornfield (27), *Full Catastrophe Living* by Jon Kabat-Zinn (14), and *Tao of Meditation* by Tsung Hwa Jou (36).

An attractive aspect of meditation is its simplicity. You can do it just about anywhere, it doesn't cost anything, your practice can

---

\* We are talking here about the stationary form of practice, either sitting or reclining, and using concentration to clear the mind. Physical forms of meditation, such as yoga and Tai Chi, also exist. See Chapter 7.

remain completely private, and there is no right or wrong way to do it. As long as your way allows you to become still and go within for a reasonable period of time, it can be effective. However, while meditation is simple, in the beginning, you may find it difficult and frustrating. Sitting quietly, doing nothing, and not thinking goes against almost everyone's cultural conditioning. A shift in perspective must eventually occur from one of the ingrained habit of believing to one of direct knowing. This happens only through consistent practice, being patient when no results seem to be forthcoming, and being persistent until the results do come.

Yet, even when the direct knowing comes, the palpable feeling associated with it is likely to fade until the next time you experience a moment of illumination. While you will grow through the accumulation of these experiences, a particular sensing of Truth and its afterglow will usually become a distant memory. Don Juan, the sorcerer-teacher* of Carlos Casteneda, often talked about how there would be lengthy periods during which Casteneda would forget the experiences he encountered during mystical states of awareness, what Don Juan called the Second Attention, until they became integrated more fully into his conscious awareness (3).

This integration can take a long time to happen. During these in-between periods, you're left with a residual feeling of what was absolutely true in the moment you encountered it; but, you also may feel somewhat abandoned. It's almost as if a wonderful new friend has disappeared just as that person entered your

---

\* The Toltec term for a spiritual master is actually, Nagual, which means *master of intent*. The Nagual is one who is completely devoid of ego and self-definition and uses the Intent of the Universe to shape reality for him (her)-self. The students also find their sense of reality changing as the Nagual helps doors of perception to open. One day, some of the students will reach a sufficient level of mastery to assume the mantle of their teacher, continuing that teacher's particular Nagual lineage, which, in many cases, has existed for centuries.

life and began to restore adventure and purpose to it. At first, when this friend leaves, dark moods or pronounced anxiety may arise. For me, the longing I spoke about earlier in my experience would come back even stronger after my initial encounters of illumination. As time went on, I realized that this longing was just another part of the awakening process.

The flip side of the passing of long, uneventful periods is the possibility of suddenly appearing, distinct changes in energy, dreaming, or any number of other experiential dimensions. In my case, a period of about six weeks materialized where every third or fourth night brought an intense energy flow that literally surged through me for hours. Its onset was usually during the hypnogogic state, immediately before falling asleep or just after waking in the morning, before I became fully conscious. At other times, it came in the middle of the night, waking me abruptly.

In all cases, my entire body seemed to be vibrating extremely rapidly, literally taking my breath away. This exquisite force was exhilarating beyond words and did not hurt me. However, on some occasions, I sensed that I was very close to the threshold of passing on. I had several dreams and visions, in the presence of this energy, of being with relatives or friends who had long since passed on. I hesitate to use the term dream, because these experiences seemed to be real events that just happened to be occurring within another level of reality. I was immensely gratified to be with these loved ones after so long without them, and I basked in the warmth of these encounters for days afterward.

Although this energy vanished as inexplicably as it had arrived, one of its effects has since stayed with me. My sleep patterns have changed significantly in that I rarely seem to have an uninterrupted night of slumber anymore. It is true that consistent meditation does promote an ongoing sense of general well-being and relaxation, but, at least for me, it has induced frequent periods of nocturnal wakefulness. On days following the nights of little sleep, I can experience the odd consequence of feeling either very little, or tremendous, vitality. It's hard to predict which condition will turn up, other than to notice that an unusually deep meditation during the night can precede a day of unusually robust vigor. Also, it may not be surprising that two or three sleep-deprived nights and low-energy days will lead to a full night of sleep.*

This description of what the energy of Love feels like once a person invites it in over a period of time is especially fitting. "You are beginning to feel the results of the transformation

> Become as empty as possible, and be ready to see where the journey will take you next, if anywhere.

process which is working from the deepest level of your being outward …You also noticed the difference when you slipped out of this unity and back into third-dimensional thinking. It felt uncomfortable and heavy and you wanted the joyous, light, lovely feeling back. This has set the tone for your learning processes … Then gradually, you began to feel the lightness creeping into other parts of your body until now you feel as though you are filled with Light. You feel so full of this wonderful substance that

---

* I don't view any of these bodily changes as medical issues (such as particular sleep disorders) to be concerned about, since I don't experience them as being harmful or maladaptive. However, I have also noticed other effects that some may interpret as being medically disturbing. The day after one particularly deep meditation, I went to the doctor for a routine exam. My blood pressure reading was extremely high, almost off the charts. The doctor was alarmed, but intuitively, this was not surprising to me because I was still sensing the residual energy from my previous day's meditation. Sure enough, this reading later proved to be an anomaly, but it still seemed to run counter to the popular notion that consistent meditation will help to lower blood pressure. Indeed, it will help over the long haul, as I have found. The point is that certain consequences of increased energy awareness may appear worrisome or counterintuitive when, in my opinion, what is really happening in the body physically, as a result, is not very well understood scientifically.

at times it almost seems as if it is pushing against your body and expanding it. You have a feeling of hollowness, as if the real you is being restricted by the boundaries of your physical being. This is a different feeling and concept for you and not always comfortable." (26)

These insights and openings of expanded awareness have fascinated me, not only because they bring the gift of feeling connected to everything, or of knowing that Reality is much grander than I had previously believed, but also because I wonder about their origin. Am I making them happen through my own will, or is a Divine actor spoon-feeding me insights when It thinks I am ready? My best understanding is that the decision to release personal will is actually required to invite these experiences. If the Human Being really is infinite, an integral part of Universal Mind consisting of Higher Self, Soul, or Divine Being, then this Greater Will that the smaller self cannot yet see must be calling the shots, as it were. The only role I play is to get my ego out of the way as best I can. That's why I have learned that to try to will a particular spiritual experience to happen again is pointless. It's all about becoming as empty as possible and being ready to see where the journey will take you next, if anywhere.

The risk does exist for those who are willful that a few glimpses of illumination will seductively draw their energy into the pursuit of special effects for their own sake, instead of the greater understanding of Love and Reality as it truly is. As I mentioned earlier, this was certainly true for me at one time. Jack Kornfield (1) sums it up this way: "Just as there is danger for a culture that ignores the process of initiation and the experiences of satori, grace, and illumination, there is also a danger in describing them in too much detail. That danger is that they will become too important in our minds, or that we will glamorize these stories and believe they are necessary in order to live a spiritual life." These openings may happen rapidly or only after years and years of practice. Remember that the purpose of the spiritual journey is not just having moments of illumination, as wonderful as they are. It is also to renew the capacity to feel Love, to help you integrate these moments into your sense of self after they happen, and eventually, to gain the spiritual maturity this will bring.

After discerning these subtleties for myself, I realized I needed to follow another level of practice, besides direct experience, to maintain my equilibrium in the world. Consciously persisting in leaving fear behind and bringing Love into my everyday living at the level of waking awareness were the means I found necessary to accomplish this. Our exploration of spiritual practice would not be complete without my sharing them with you.

To that end, you will find many specific opportunities here to begin being in the world in a new way that promotes inner peace and fulfillment. The focus will be on how to weave these ideas into your daily life to release fear and raise the level of your consciousness.

### Fifteen Practical Ways to Release Fear

These methods are really intended to be reminders to help you once you have made the decision to expand the boundaries of your experience. It can be bewildering at times, as you suddenly become aware of buried feelings and more subtle levels of consciousness than you have been accustomed to encountering. It can also be frustrating during the periods where nothing seems to be happening, and you find yourself asking, "What am I doing wrong?" Having these reminders will help you keep your eye on the prize and avoid getting bogged down in fear and unproductive self-judgment. They are also highly beneficial for anyone to practice, even people having no particular desire for spiritual growth.

> Leaving fear behind and bringing Love into everyday living is essential for maintaining balance in the world.

One more bit of advice. It's not necessary, nor is it recommended, to try to keep all of these in your mind each and every day. Any of these methods can be explored, one or two at a time, in whatever order and speed you choose. The sincere exploration of just one will be transformational and will naturally lead you to the others. Also, some are naturally related to each other, often making the same points in different ways. After a while, you will find yourself coming back to each one over and over again in various life situations. Before long, a new perspective on living will emerge from within.

- *Be Persistent*
  This can be a tricky one at first. *Do not try hard, and do not do more.* You are not accomplishing an objective; you are actually being asked to do less than you ever have done (40). How can you persist, yet not try hard, especially at doing less? Persisting here means quietly abiding with your genuine desire and intent, not exerting your will to succeed. In this case, your intent is to know your inner self and experience the more subtle levels of being that exist underneath and between the gross perceptions of reality that we all know. This requires learning how to quiet the mind, be still, and pay attention. In the beginning, that takes willingness to accept the paradox that doing nothing leads to having everything, until you can glimpse it for yourself.

- *Be Patient*
  Go easy on yourself. Having a plan with a timetable isn't going to help you grow spiritually. Be patient, even if you know you are caught in a bout of drama or nothing seems to be happening. Balance your desire with the knowledge that the speed of your progress, whatever it may be, is perfectly appropriate for your needs at any given point in time.
  From a higher perspective, remember that sometimes "God is slow" (5,11,40). Your role is to choose your desired end-state, but not to control the particulars of

how or when it will come into existence. Once you have given your sincere intent for a particular result, you must let the Universe manifest it appropriately (see Appendix A—A Selected Channeling). Universal order is realized when the changes you are

> The spiritual path is one of self-discovery, the knowing, little by little, of the Self as infinite, as well as specific.

initiating through the power of your intent are woven together harmoniously with the intent of all others around you. Your pure intent will be realized, but Spirit has the big picture of how it all must come together, moment by moment. It may happen through a series of events that never would have occurred to you, but that are nonetheless perfect for you and everyone else. This is one of the meanings of the expression, "Let go and let God."

A final word on patience. As you live increasingly in the present moment you will reach a point where it is actually not necessary. The term patience implies a subtle tension from having to tolerate a condition of current lack until it is satisfied at a future point. In the Now (29), the only point in which anything is really happening, past and future do not exist and, ultimately, no patience is required. "Infinite patience brings immediate results" (40). That is, being in the present moment brings the experience of Being, where one knows complete fulfillment directly.

I often see this principle manifested in small but meaningful ways whenever I can truly accept the present moment as it is. While in a slow moving line at the supermarket checkout, for instance, as soon as I completely let go of all thoughts and feelings of willfulness to hurry things along, I seem to find myself sailing through another register that has just opened up. Pay attention to these so-called coincidences, and try to notice the correlation to your state of being at these times.

- *Honor Yourself*
  You may hear from others and perhaps your own ego, that paying attention to your spiritual growth is tantamount to being selfish. While a sincere quest for expanded consciousness may make people around you uneasy, and compel them to reexamine their own habits and beliefs, empowering yourself to discover who you truly are is your highest pursuit in life.

It's unlikely you will give away all your possessions and find yourself moving to a cave, even if another is afraid that you will decide to take such actions. At the same time, you will be changing, although it is likely that you will make compromises with significant others in certain situations out of respect for how much change they can handle. But, regardless of your

> Take responsibility for the world you see, without falling into the trap of feeling guilty because your current world falls short of the one you now know you could be seeing.

discernment in any given circumstance, it's important to drop the hesitation or guilt over being selfish in pursuing your growth. Remember not to hold yourself to another's current level of understanding, or their fear of what is as yet unknown to them, if it is now appropriate for you to embrace new experiences and ideas. Certainly, you must honor the path of all people, but remember that you are included in the set of all people.

Release the false sense of responsibility that is generally accepted as a fact of life by everyone else. As Don Miguel Ruiz (13) said, you needn't take anything personally because everyone is dreaming his or her own experience; it actually has nothing to do with you. It is truly liberating to realize that only your Intent matters. As long as you are doing your best, from whatever level of understanding you presently have, literally nothing else can be done.

Don't let the judgments of others about your choices for growth provoke a need to defend or justify yourself. Yes, this can be challenging, once it begins to appear as if you now have a foot in two worlds, and you must learn how to unite the two. Once again, persist. To paraphrase the quote by Marcus Aurelius (23) that opens this chapter, reclaim the energy you have lost by ceasing to give your power away to others, and Love yourself before anyone. That is wise, not selfish.

- *Feel Your Emotions*
One of the main pathways to getting beyond the ego to the level of your true Being is through your emotions. Most of us have painful emotions—anger, guilt, and so on—from past events in our lives that we continue to carry with us. We also experience pain from new emotions as new situations arise, and since we do not consciously recognize them, they add to our accumulated burden of past pain. In the present moment, we either relive actual emotions from time to time, or if we have buried them, we experience a general sense of anxiety or ennui instead.

Realize that you have the power to observe these emotions instead of turning away from them. The simple act of observing whatever you are experiencing, *without judgment,* in the present moment is all that is necessary to move past the pain. You don't have to understand the genesis or historical detail of the emotions to resolve them. All you need is to bring the light of your attention to bear in the Now, whether the issues arose in the past or in this moment (29).[*,†,6]

Also, notice the subtle, but very important, difference between emotions and feelings (40). Emotions are a product of the ego, while feelings come from the Soul. All emotions arise from various forms of fear and, like the ego, are ultimately not real. Feelings—Joy and Love among them—on the other hand, are genuine and arise from infinite and eternal Being. When you become

---

[*] Eckhart Tolle covers this practice very eloquently in *The Power of Now*, and because this is such a powerful practice, it is highly recommended reading. Also, see the meditation, *I Love Myself*, under Thirteen Ways to Enrich Your Meditations in Chapter 7.

[†] I do recognize that this sounds very simplistic, or too good to be true. How can one bypass all of the hard work in therapy required to bring powerful emotions, long buried in the subconscious, to the surface so they may be released? Having experienced both long years of therapy and the practice of just being present with difficult emotions, I can say that having the guidance of a skilled and caring therapist does have value. However, I believe that any healing arrived at in the therapeutic process is ultimately a result of the same practice of presence that Tolle and others describe. In fact, a recently developed approach to helping patients cope with unusually powerful emotions, dialectical behavior therapy, "has become one of the most popular new psychotherapies in a generation." A key element of its success is to help patients "notice when their emotions begin to stir, allow themselves to feel the storm whip up, then let it pass—all without doing anything." If therapy, on the other hand, becomes some sort of internal witch-hunt or an intellectual exercise, then you will gain no value. As far as the practice of presence being too simplistic is concerned, you will discover that all spiritual truth is exquisitely clear-cut, even though it may sometimes be difficult to understand conceptually or to consistently embody in the world. I would also refer you to Ken Wilber's book, *No Boundary* (25), for a wonderful explanation of the different levels of human consciousness and their primary avenues of attention and healing.

conscious of feeling from the level of the Soul—at the birth of a child or at the death of a loved one, as two universal and unmistakable examples—this difference is clear.

- *Realize You Are Making Choices*
  Thoughts and words have creative power. Beliefs are the thoughts you give focused and sustained commitment to, and they form the mental energy that you set in motion to eventually find expression in the world. The totality of your beliefs literally determines what you physically experience. It is very important to understand that, despite what you think

  > Eventually, evidence will materialize in your life that will enable you to tie what you have changed internally to your external environment.

  you see, nothing is being done to you, and the conditions in your life, good or bad, aren't the result of random outside forces or God's rewards or punishments. Your ego is manufacturing a personal dream of the world. Like those of most people, the dream is usually one of suffering in its many forms (13).

  Hell is not the pit of eternal damnation so many have envisioned. Hell is a state of existence the mind generates, right here, right now. It naturally follows that reaching the Kingdom of Heaven is also possible at any moment, not only upon death. Seeing more of Heaven is done not through a process of accumulation—of knowledge, good deeds, or divine dispensation—but through a process of removal. It requires the stripping away of the negative beliefs about Life that have become burdensome attachments and habits over a long period of time.

  Only one person can fundamentally change your experience of Life, and that's you! It's your choice. This is one of the most difficult and liberating aspects of spiritual growth to grasp. Difficult, because it takes patience and persistence to wait for a new reality to manifest as you practice observing and changing deeply held or previously unnoticed beliefs. Liberating, because, eventually, evidence will materialize in your life that will enable you to tie what you have changed internally to your external environment. It bears remembering that this requires the commitment to take responsibility for the world you see, without falling into the trap of feeling guilty because your current world falls short of the one you now know you could be seeing.

The bottom line is that your sincere desire and effort to change your prevailing thoughts and words is the engine that will lead to a different experience. Begin to pay close attention to what you think and say. Do you find yourself automatically identifying with beliefs like, "You can't trust anybody these days," or "I don't deserve to be happy," or "At my age, things really start falling apart"? Can you acknowledge any correlation between your most cherished beliefs and your reality? If you want a different outcome, use your intent to allow Spirit to bring the changes you desire; but, remember to be patient. Standing on the shoulders of the teachers referenced in Chapter 9, let me share a powerful statement of intent you can give to the Universe.

> Being that Spirit is all there is of me, I give my pure intent for the effortless manifestation of all of the good that is already mine, in full measure, allowing Spirit to provide abundance, health, and peace in my experience, to meet all of my needs and desires, in perfect harmony with the Universe and God's Will.

Of course, you may use this same form for any statement

of intent. The key is becoming aware of beliefs that are incongruent with the outcomes you desire, and then using your sincere intent to change them (5,11,13,24).

- *Release Judgment*
  There is only what is so. How you experience what is so depends on the definitions you give. Whether something has value, or an event or person is good or bad, is your subjective evaluation derived from the information you happen to possess. However, usually, you don't have the necessary perspective to judge anything appropriately. Do you really understand why a person acted in a way you consider to be improper? Can you see the big picture that would show you what lesson that person is to learn or their role as a catalyst in the learning of other people?

  It is certainly wise to be discerning (see below). But, before you jump to conclusions about something, know that holding judgments about what is so, and not accepting it as it is, represents the main reason that the experience of what is so feels so much like suffering. Accept what is, and then take whatever action is fitting: change it, leave it, or embrace it (29). Leave the judgment to others. Let go of the many faces of drama: gossip, jealousy, impatience, playing the victim, and so on (13,15).

  In the larger arenas of mass events—politics, war, natural disaster, etc.—"Stay above the fray" (11). The same principle of not seeing fully what is so applies at this level, too. Remember to release judgment of others—events, people, or things—above all, so that you may avoid judging yourself.

- *Be Discerning*
  Discernment is simply the acknowledgment of what is so. It is not the same as judgment, which places a value on something, either positive or negative, usually based

on incomplete information. Once you have taken note of something without the biased filters of judgment, you will, more likely than not, respond to it

> You don't need to know anything to experience yourself as you truly are.

appropriately. Being spiritual does not mean being a doormat or being stupid (5,40), but it does mean being aware. You will know what level of integrity someone is demonstrating, because you are making it your practice to summon the integrity that resides within you. In some encounters, it may be that your highest response is to say no, leave a situation, put another in an uncomfortable position, or physically defend yourself—*all without passing judgment.*

Discernment is also necessary as far as the ideas you are entertaining in your mind and, ultimately, accepting as beliefs. My own bias is to be skeptical of people and organizations that believe they have all the answers, such as political parties, activist groups, or organized religions. To be sure, I am painting with a wide brush; many sincere people have done socially valuable work within these institutions. Many groups admirably perform services that society would otherwise forego. However, a lack of tolerance for ideas outside the organization's orthodoxy, or an agenda that is less than transparent, often exists. Why limit your curiosity and knowledge to the boundaries of what the group will accept? Joining a team of like-minded people to accomplish a worthy objective is commendable. However, take care not to concede your internal knowing to any group's, or any person's, beliefs.

When it comes to listening to the arguments of experts, realize that experts rarely agree on any issue. Look closely at their positions to determine whether you can take them at face value or whether they are predisposed by an ingrained doctrine or conflict of interest. Also, don't be intimidated by authorities that say you can't consider yourself well informed unless you have earned a PhD or have an expert's grasp of a particular specialty. Nonsense! You are intelligent enough to listen to different experts, weigh their arguments, and discard any hidden agendas they may have. Then decide for yourself. Of course, always be open to new information and the possibility that you may decide to change your mind.

Above all, always remember that you don't need to know anything to experience yourself as you truly are. As Eckhart Tolle reminds us, "There is nothing you need to understand before you can become present (29)." Be discerning when others say that only through their concepts or requirements can you achieve enlightenment or salvation. At best, theirs is only another way to bring you to the point of finding your own freedom on your own terms.

▪ *Take Care of Yourself*

The self is multidimensional, much grander than can be imagined from our three-dimensional perspective. Still, we can say that the self consists basically of mind, body, and soul—all of which are revealed in their true fullness through growing spiritually. Up to this point, we have been largely involved with changing our beliefs (mind) about the nature of things to pierce the "veil of illusion" that separates us from our true being (soul). However, we really haven't concerned ourselves much with the body.

In actuality, the body is flawless, doing its best to represent your divine perfection in time and space. Naturally, this truth is very difficult to accept given that most everyone sees evidence completely to the contrary. We suffer disease and injury, we age relatively quickly, and we usually die well before reaching one hundred years of age. Nonetheless, the basic reason we experience the body as less than perfect, and don't see the more of it that there is to see, is, in a word, beliefs. As always, the thoughts the mind incessantly dwells on eventually become manifest in physical reality (23). If yours are negative thoughts grounded in the past (guilt, anger, etc.) or future (worry, fear, etc.), then your body, cells, and all, will literally take you at your word and express it tangibly.

*Creating Health* by Deepak Chopra, MD (8) explains very well the mind, body, and spirit connection and makes a compelling case for reexamining what you always took for granted about medicine, as well as the body. *Anatomy of the Spirit* by Caroline Myss (2) shows us how health problems really begin as nonphysical imbalances of energy that result from negative beliefs about ourselves or traumatic experiences we have buried. In *Diet For a New America*, John Robbins (9) also insightfully challenges

> Your bodywork will be motivated less by ego than by a genuine desire to know all aspects of yourself at their highest possible levels.

the conventional wisdom about health from the standpoint of nutrition. Spiritual growth will have a positive impact on your health that won't only be the result of reducing stress through meditation and the like, but will also come about through purposeful changes you will make in your daily habits. You may become a vegetarian or take up running, but you will be motivated less by ego considerations, than by a genuine desire to know all aspects of yourself at their highest possible levels.

Your spiritual practice and bodywork together will

lead to discernable benefits that will help you dislodge old, shop-worn beliefs, and you will establish a virtuous circle. Nothing is irreversible. Begin to do what you can do from whatever your current position of health is. If you're not doing everything you think you could be doing, don't fall into the trap of doing nothing. Any sincere step in the direction of better health, which is just another way of knowing who you truly are, is worthwhile.

Also, don't fall into the trap of believing that the body is somehow unspiritual or must be transcended to know yourself as a divine being. In fact, just the opposite is true. Your body, often the source of so much dissatisfaction and worry, is actually your gateway to the Divine. It is true that you are not your body, in the sense of physical limitation or decay. But, the Infinite and Eternal continually shine through your physical form, waiting to be experienced through that form, if you choose to pay attention.

In his Sermon on the Body (29), Eckhart Tolle teaches us "not to fight against the body, for in doing so you are fighting against your own reality. You *are* your body. The body that you can see and touch is only a thin illusory veil. Underneath it lays the invisible inner body, the doorway into Being, into Life unmanifested." The phrase "going within" to find stillness and peace really means just that—turning your attention inward to your body to become aware of the "animating Life Force" inside that you have forgotten existed.

The denial of physical pleasure for the sake of spiritual purity, so common in the major religions, and the main reason we often dismiss the sacredness of the body, is unfortunate, to say the least. Many spiritual seekers through the ages renounced their bodily needs and the emotions associated with them, especially those having to do with sex, and only brought themselves and others unnecessary suffering. In Spiritual Emergency (see Chapter 8), we see evidence of the problems that can occur when people reawaken to the feelings and sensations of the physical world after years of living in seclusion, committed only to spiritual discipline. Romantic relationships and sexual expression are examples of these challenges.

Even within our own culture, we endure much misery because of pressure to conform to moral codes that warn against enjoying the body in a sexual way. Our collective sophistication still masks a strong puritanical undercurrent that assigns shame to physical expressions of love, while we tolerate, or even embrace, messages of violence and death. Accordingly, we see that our society's sexual dialog is not very sophisticated at all, consisting mainly of stilted stereotypes or attention-getting caricatures. Many of us grow up confused by the inconsistency between these messages and what we feel naturally deep inside ourselves. We often spend our adult years trying to fill the emptiness that exists underneath the artificial moral edifice we believe we must maintain.

What we miss in all our defensiveness is the fact that sexual energy is every bit as sacred as anything we traditionally ascribe to being Divine. Sexual energy is one way the energy of Spirit manifests itself in the body. It is revealing to observe that during or after especially deep meditations, along with the feelings of great peace and well-being, sexual energy can also be very apparent. It seems that at the profound level of Being, loving sexuality and peace go together, while at the superficial level of protocol, restrictive morality and defense go together. It's not difficult to imagine which path leads to health and which leads to dysfunction.

Of course, appreciating the miracle that is your body in tangible ways is not an endorsement for hedonistic or reckless practices, which are every bit as limiting as renouncing the body. Pain and suffering can also materialize by taking advantage of another person sexually, insulting the body by using drugs, eating without any regard for the body's welfare, or through any number of other unconscious activities. Try to make lifestyle choices based on your inner integrity, not based on the opposite extremes of rigid moral codes and instant gratification. The decision to give up meat, for instance, can come from deep within and be spiritually liberating, even though others might interpret it as a form of physical denial. At the same time, enjoying the sensations of the body on a whim—whether having sex or an ice cream sundae—is not a spiritual detriment, even though others may see you as not being true to your stated values.

Take the time to value the divine intelligence of your bodily functions at work within you. Follow your body's lead, and don't resist what it is communicating. If it is telling you to go to the bathroom, then go. Don't wait until you finish a supposedly critical task; put your body first. Know that through the practice of loving your body enough to honor its needs, it will return that love in the form of greater physical and spiritual well-being.

You may also communicate your love to your body each day to reinforce a virtuous circle of health and vitality. When you arise in the morning, say aloud this earnest expression of appreciation:[*]

> My dear body, thank you for having the intent and purpose to identify my Divine Being perfectly, right here where I am. I authorize you to release any and all impediments to your perfect function so that I may know you as you truly are in your divine perfection.

---

[*]    Adapted from Raj (40).

Give your body consistent messages of gratitude, rather than those of frustration and fear. Then watch the power of your intent become manifest as your body responds in kind.

- *Listen to Yourself*

  Looking, really looking, at the incredible complexity and wonder of nature will lead the intellect to the logical conclusion that there must be far more to be known than it is capable of absorbing rationally. It is at the limits of the intellect that faith comes in. For if you know there is more knowledge available beyond these limits, and you aren't seeing it by conventional means, it then becomes a question of whether you will decide to open your eyes to your own direct experience.

  Pay attention, and then trust the process. Accept on faith that beholding the Truth, the way things really work, requires mastery, which you (and I) do not yet have. Still, that the Truth is all there is, and that what you are seeing is not the Truth, is no less a fact. Know that, little by little, your perspective will change as you allow additional information to enter.

  As you begin to pay attention, look between the lines in your life. Notice the so-called coincidences that seem to appear at just the right time. Notice your dreams and thoughts. Where did they come from, and what are they saying to you? Trust your first impressions, resisting the ingrained habit to push them away, telling yourself that it must have been your imagination. There is wisdom here. Be grateful for it.

- *Let in Joy*

  Joy is always present, but you must let it in. The world today conspires to keep the Joy out in the name of sophistication and propriety. Not only is this denial a shame, it's also insane. If Joy is hidden, take notice of what brings you Joy and revel in it.

In my case, I'm an unabashed dog lover. From childhood I think I always knew this but I never really noticed it until our dog, Frosty, joined us in 1999. The books written and research done (16) on the well-known human-canine bond are illuminating, but the quality of a personal encounter with a dog goes beyond words, if you really abandon

> Begin to do things that lead you to challenge your long-held definitions that have circumscribed your self-image.

yourself to it. I often find myself asking as I look at my dog's face and watch her behavior, just what makes me feel so joyful. I could say it's the hint of mischief in her smile or her complete lack of pretense that I am now arguing we humans should adopt. But ultimately, it's a whole that is far more compelling than any of the parts that would occur to me.

Find your Joy in whatever form has meaning for you, and let it in. Do it now, regardless of what others think or what else is going on around you. Not only does your spiritual growth depend on experiencing Joy, but your physical and mental well-being depend on it, too.

- *Stretch Your Boundaries*
Do things you wouldn't ordinarily do, especially those things that allow you to challenge the long-held definitions that have circumscribed your self-image. Stretching takes some degree of vigilance, because as opportunities present themselves, ingrained behaviors often inhibit action just as it becomes apparent that an opportunity exists (5). Let me illustrate this notion with a personal experience.

During the summer of 2000, I attended the premier trade show of our industry on the West Coast, along with other people from my company. One evening, a group of us strolled along the restaurant district near the convention center and found a nice café setting outdoors to eat dinner. Shortly after we placed our orders, a disheveled, somewhat disoriented man, whom I assume was homeless, approached our table and gruffly asked for money. I was immediately torn. On one hand, I wanted to act on my recently established conviction that no person has more value than another does by looking this man in the eye, talking to him, and even giving him a few bucks for a meal. (Let's set aside for now the social debate on whether giving homeless people money is productive.) On the other hand, the people at my table were all ignoring this guy, waiting for him to go away, which he eventually did. I knew that if I took the culturally improper action of following my desire, I would risk offending people I work with, some of whom were senior executives in the company.

Now, for all I know, I may have been selling my associates short; they could very well have been feeling as I did. The point is that I failed to honor my integrity and take action. At that moment, ingrained social convention was more important to me. Later, walking back to the hotel, I was lost in thoughts of self-recrimination, feeling that I let myself down. I silently asked Spirit to give me another opportunity.

Two days later, after an all-night flight back east, the plane landed at 6:30 a.m. I grabbed my car, anxious to get home. Just outside the airport, I rolled onto the entrance ramp of the expressway and noticed a broken-down vehicle with a man next to it waving his arms. Without realizing it, I slowed down, my first thought to offer him the use of my cell phone. As he approached my car, he seemed very worried that I would drive off in fear, possibly because we were strangers and he was agitated.

After calming down, he told me that he had called for a tow truck, but the initial charge was fifteen dollars, and he had no cash. That he was sincere and needed help I had no doubt. So, again, without much thought, I opened my wallet and found that I had fourteen dollars left. Close enough. After I gave him the money, he looked at me for a moment and then softly said, "Bless you, brother."

I can tell you that, as I drove away, I experienced an incredible feeling of connection and Joy that I never got before from accomplishments or things. I get a lump in my throat just writing about it now. For me, this act was the gift of Tikkun ha-olam (the Jewish term for healing the world) applied in real life (15). The experience of it showed me that the primary recipient of this gift was not the person I had helped. It was I, who had received the gift of Love ten times over by giving it away. Other compelling examples of challenging who you think you are, are described by Victor Sanchez in his book *The Teachings of Don Carlos* (38), one of which includes a high-ranking government official who sold newspapers on the street in Mexico City to wake up from his dream of self-importance. Questioning and, where appropriate, rejecting conventional notions of propriety, especially as they apply to you, is a sure and powerful way to foster spiritual growth.

- *Don't Run Away*
  Don't retreat from the world. Use the people and events in your world as openings to grow and practice. Begin to see difficult people and situations as your teachers (2). Know that, in actuality, you are bringing them to you for reasons that are yours to discover. If you find yourself repeatedly in a certain type of relationship, or in various circumstances that all have in common conditions that provoke your anger, for example, you are being invited to

look closer. There is a lesson waiting for you to learn that once recognized, will allow its release. Don't sit on a mountaintop looking for truth; the marketplace and relationships are the crucibles for spiritual growth (1,40). That is where you will find your highest understanding and have the opportunity to illuminate the way for others by what you have learned.

> Don't sit on a mountaintop looking for truth. Use your existing relationships as opportunities to transform your beliefs and emotions.

At the same time, accept change. If the world is presenting you with an ongoing parade of difficult situations, when you finally see their lesson clearly, you may need to alter your life in some way to move on. Inherent in the process of consciously opening your eyes is transformation, not only of spiritual awareness, but also of beliefs, emotions, and tangible aspects of existence. Generally, you may choose the speed at which this change occurs, but eventually, it will happen because the same situations will keep coming until you notice and face them.

Ultimately, the fact is that nothing is static in the Universe. Accepting this Law of Impermanence is a major step toward spiritual maturity; however, it does run counter to our craving for stability in everything. We want our significant others to always be the same people we knew way back when. We demand that our career always moves forward and our economy continually expands. We need to know that our society's values and institutions are rock solid, impervious to unorthodox ideas. It sounds trite, but change is unavoidable. Once you accept that you are literally creating the change, even if you don't yet see this, you will be on your way to the freedom that comes with taking responsibility for it.

- *Keep Out Noise*
Watch what you allow into your mind (24). So much of the stimuli from our postmodern environment is a continual stream of chaotic noise. Ubiquitous commercials, e-mail spam, and telemarketing calls desperately try to get our attention in increasingly outrageous ways. Politicians stay on message by incessantly repeating their extreme positions and disingenuously utilizing fear to advance their agendas. Television programming, especially the news, brings the most degrading stupidity of which we humans are capable into our homes in graphic detail, in real time, from anywhere in the world. The car at the red light next to us spews songs of rape and death, full blast from its 800-watt audio system.

We have gradually become so inured to this onslaught that we meekly, even unwittingly, accept the very real impediment it presents to our experience of well-being. *Notice this rubbish!* Then honestly ask yourself whether watching the latest terrorist attack over and over again on the news, or seeing the bad guy's head getting blown off in slow motion, is really worth your attention. If you think this is being needlessly uptight and all of the gratuitous noise is harmless, remember that your mind captures every image, whether or not you realize it. Even though nothing is irreversible, does it make sense to allow this stuff to keep accumulating inside you? I challenge you to see what happens when you decide to let the phone ring, turn off the TV, and roll up the car window. Not only will you reacquaint yourself with a sense of calm you have disregarded, but in a very important way, you will also loosen the grip on society held by those who depend on everyone's acquiescence for their power and control.

By all means, enjoy fully the spice of politics and entertainment, and make sure that you are well-informed about the news, both from a contemporary and an historical perspective. Dysfunction portrayed dramatically, even violence, if it is used in proportion, has always been an essential part of cultural substance and richness. Profane humor, too. Look to a wide variety of sources for your information and amusement, and, of course, deny access whenever you feel your integrity is being violated. Begin to reclaim responsibility for the quality of your internal territory, which, after all, rests on the wisdom of your choices.

- *Simplify Your Life*
  Having and enjoying the finer things in life—a beautiful home, clothes that you find pleasing, a superb musical instrument, if you are a musician—are not unspiritual and are every bit as valid a part of the experiential landscape as anything else is. Just don't become identified with any of it (29). Ultimately, real wealth is found in knowing and experiencing your Self as you truly are, to your greatest potential, in all facets of your existence.

  Therefore, have fun with it all, but don't get bogged down in the hyper-acquisitiveness that traps so many of us these days. The more stuff you have, the more you must keep track of and maintain, and the more burdensome your stuff becomes. Gladly release what no longer has meaning for you, and don't look back. Reduce the unnecessary encumbrances so that the more unfettered enjoyment of what really matters in your life right Now becomes possible.

- *Begin Where You Are*
  When you find yourself slipping back into ego and drama, and you know it, see it clearly and then move on. In the very next instant, your error is in the past, and the past doesn't exist except in your own mind. There is absolutely no need to bring guilt forward. The only thing relevant

is what you do right now. So, in this moment, you now have the opportunity to make a different choice. You have at least as many chances as the present moment is deep, which is, in a word, infinite. Always start from Now.

Let me say a final word on the daily practice of leaving fear behind and its possible effect on conscious experience. As you patiently persist in practicing the release of fear, while also inviting the direct experience of Love, you may encounter shifts in perception that can be truly amazing, although difficult to grasp. Like the spiritual insights

> Resist explaining away what doesn't seem to fit into everyone's definition of *normal.* Be open to your true nature, and have fun with it.

and feelings of deep peace I spoke of earlier, these glimpses of a larger Reality will also cause you to reassess what you think you know. I can share a few personal examples, one during a meditation, one while walking through the cafeteria at work, and another shortly after waking one morning.

In the first instance, I was on a cross-country flight to the West Coast. When I grew tired of reading, I decided to pass the time by meditating, and, before long, I reached a familiar state of deep relaxation. But then, I was suddenly amazed to find myself (my conscious awareness) outside the plane, flying along with it. I could look down at the earth's features below and enjoy a much wider field of vision than if I had been looking out the window from my seat. Still, this visual awareness had a different quality to it than what is usually produced by light sensed through the eyes and interpreted by the brain. It was as if I were dreaming, the world backlit with an ethereal glow; but, in this case, my dream was the tangible world outside at that moment in time. After what seemed only a matter of moments, I was back in my seat marveling at this exhilarating instant of enhanced perception.

The second occurrence was no less extraordinary. At work during lunch one day, I approached the salad bar having no other thought than to get my food, sit down, and eat. As I prepared my salad, without warning, my sense of smell became extremely acute, so much so that I thought to myself, "this is what being a dog must be like."* Instantly, I could detect the most exquisitely subtle odors—smells within smells within smells. It was at once thrilling and overwhelming. Think of Dorothy stepping out of her front door from the black-and-white world of Kansas into the Technicolor of Oz. An entire world of astonishing olfactory perception had inexplicably opened up very briefly and then disappeared as quickly as it came.

In the third case, I had just awoken one morning and continued to lie in bed with my eyes still shut, feeling unusually well rested. I slowly became aware that I could see the room, illuminated by the soft light of dawn filtering through the window shade, even though my eyes were completely closed. Objects—a desk, a chair, a bookcase—were all visible to me in every sense, and as I passed my hand in front of my face, I could see its detailed form as well, not just its shadow. Intrigued, I opened and closed my eyes to make sure they had actually been closed in the first place, and to see whether the minimal level of illumination in the room had really been bright enough to explain my vision. After a few minutes of this, the enhanced sight faded, and then when I closed my eyes, I could see nothing other than the vague presence of sunlight. My curiosity was satisfied that I had experienced something remarkable.

---

* Jack Kornfield relates a similar experience of his in *A Path With Heart* (27), during a discussion of the many possible side effects of "the spiritual roller coaster." He recalls a morning living as a Buddhist monk in Asia when, "my nose became like that of the most sensitive dog. As I walked down the street of a small village, every two feet there was a different smell: something being washed, fertilizer in the garden, new paint on a building, the lighting of a charcoal fire in a Chinese store, the cooking in the next window. It was an extraordinary experience of moving through the world attuned to all the possibilities of smell."

My point in relating these anecdotes to you is that the expansion of consciousness may take different and varied forms as Love emerges. We need not approach it with trepidation, but instead, embrace it as an adventure in self-discovery. Should you come across these wonderful clues about who you really are as you become more Loving, you may find yourself asking whether what you thought just happened actually happened. Even so, remember that this kind of response is a conditioned one emanating from years of explaining away what doesn't seem to fit into everyone's definition of what is normal. These experiences may not adhere to the norm, which is simply the standard set of perceptions most people currently accept as valid, but they are natural. Be open to your true nature, and have fun with it.

## Seven Practical Ways to Bring Love into Your Life and the World

To reinforce the point made earlier, bringing your inner knowing to your daily activity is essential to your spiritual growth. Releasing the old habits of fear and negativity is done through allowing whatever Love you can muster, in whatever form, to flow within everyday situations and relationships.

> It is in the movement of God's Love that your world becomes illuminated, and in its idleness that you remain in the dark.

Again, this is not a religious or moral exercise, and it is not about what you will be doing for others. Your sole purpose is to awaken from your personal dream of suffering, comfortably if possible, and by doing so, automatically help to lessen the intensity of the world's collective dream.

Another great analogy (40) helps make this clear. Picture yourself as a garden hose. The spigot has been turned on and water, fully pressurized, is now ready to be sprayed in any direction. All you need to do is to squeeze the nozzle at the end of hose. By now, perhaps, you have figured out that the water in the hose is really the Love of God that resides in you. But, you may not have realized that, unless you squeeze the nozzle and let it out, you won't feel it. It is in the movement of God's Love that your world becomes illuminated, and in its idleness that you remain in the dark.

Love has many forms of expression (we can squeeze the nozzle in many ways, in many directions). We explore a few here for you to begin to express each day. Many of the books reviewed in Chapter 9 go further in covering all of these and more. They are also inherent in the ways to release fear mentioned above. Again, be patient and persist.

- *Forgiveness*
  We often think of forgiveness as a gift one person gives to another. In a sense, if you forgive me for some transgression, you are letting me off the proverbial hook, granting me permission to get out of "guilt jail." A closer look, however, reveals this belief to be a misconception. Forgiveness is not something you bestow on someone else; it's something you do for yourself.

  Forgiveness is actually about letting go of internal toxins that only promote and prolong your suffering, regardless of what anyone else says or does.

  > Place a premium on maintaining your inner peace. Use foregiveness to do this.

  If someone has done you wrong, you will probably feel upset, even outraged, if the offense was truly awful. But, after the initial wave of anger comes and goes, a very important choice is always there, silently waiting to be made whenever you are ready. You can actually decide to separate any actions you need to take from your painful emotions, *and then release the emotions.*

  This seems almost impossibly difficult to do, and granted, the more pain that is present, the more counterintuitive and radical this seems. What could possibly motivate someone to forgive when he or she has been hurt badly and wants justice? To borrow from a famous campaign slogan, "It's the anger, stupid." This succinct phrase reminds us that only an individual's internal state governs his or her personal experience of well-being. Carrying around the baggage of anger and thoughts of revenge will simply bring you more misery, not the justice you are seeking. Once you understand this basic truth, you will begin to place a premium on maintaining your inner peace and use forgiveness frequently as an effective tool to remove any impediments to its continuance. And, ironically, your newfound clarity will allow you to respond with complete appropriateness to all facets of a challenging situation, especially ones that your anger may have kept hidden from you.

It is usually easier to begin a practice of forgiveness with smaller issues or events that occurred well in the past. Perhaps you have some residual anger toward a parent who is now gone or a sibling who treated you badly as a child. Would it not be worth a try to let the anger go now? If that is too much, maybe you can start with something as small as the irritation you feel when a co-worker interrupts you in mid-sentence during a meeting. By consciously making the choice to forgive, in whatever form, you will be rewarded with the relief of no longer having to be a victim. And, ultimately, your forgiveness will be a gift, one that you give for the collective healing of humanity.

- *Gratitude*

Many of us growing up in middle-class America can remember our mothers at mealtime admonishing us to be thankful for our food because, after all, "there are children starving in India." Well, yes, someone always seems to be worse off than we are, and we had better thank our lucky stars lest the fates take offense at our ungratefulness. In other words, we usually assume a defensive posture when it comes to being grateful. Either we wait until we are in a serious predicament and promise to do whatever it takes forevermore to show our thanks, or we whistle past the graveyard, thinking how fortunate it is that we didn't end up like that poor schlep. We may also find ourselves swimming against a steady current of vague dissatisfaction as we continually strive to keep achieving, acquiring, and attaining in our modern culture. It's just as likely, however, that gratitude doesn't really enter our thoughts very often.

If this is a shame, it is also a tremendous opportunity for any of us who decide to give at least some of our attention regularly to simply *being* grateful. Why? Because, when you are in a sincere state of consciously appreciating something, you will automatically invite the feelings of Love and Joy, at a deep level within (40). What you appreciate can be anything, a person, a pet, a tree in the backyard, or even a supposedly inanimate object, such as the water cascading across your body in the shower, keeping you warm and making you clean. At an even more basic level, you are never without the countless blessings of nature waiting for the Joy in their valuing to be uncovered. Ultimately, you can stop and realize that *you are alive*, and that your present circumstances, no matter what they may be, are only temporary, but that *you will always exist* (5).

The point is that gratitude is another tool that is always available to you for transforming your experience of Reality. Indeed, it takes persistence and a willingness to throw out the window the conventional wisdom that says, "I can't be satisfied until I have this or that, or until such and such happens." Once again, conventional wisdom is anything but wise. The truth is that *being* grateful without reservation or requirement helps change your inner state to one of harmony, and inner harmony is what removes the impediments that prevent the Universe from manifesting more easily what you desire (see Appendix A). To *have* the means to *do* what you want, *be* grateful first.

- *Humility*
  Unpretentiousness, modesty, and amenability are attributes we usually ascribe to one who is humble. True, a person practicing humility will likely demonstrate these noble characteristics, but

> When you turn your attention to the practice of humility, you begin to reclaim lost energy.

there is even more to this expression of Love. Very simply, humility comes from the genuine recognition that all humans, regardless of appearances, are of equal value to the Universe. Put another way, our limited perception is not nearly sufficient to allow us to place a relative value on anyone. In the eyes of God, whose sweep of vision is not confined by perception, all things have purpose for the evolution of the whole, and therefore, all have value in bringing that purpose to fruition. In a Divine context, no one is better than another is, and the one we may perceive as inferior may actually be a key factor in the playing out of a complex set of events involving many people, in many places, across a long period of time.

For most of us, when we encounter someone of a lower station in society, or one who is acting ignorantly, ego-centered thoughts tend to reflexively materialize. Almost without knowing it, an inner voice whispers self-congratulatory praise about our superior judgment, our harder work ethic, or our better upbringing. Well, you might ask, "If I don't aspire to be better than anyone else, won't I lose my motivation to succeed and embody values which are important to me in the world?"

First, you should know that humility, aside from giving you a more dignified demeanor, has a very practical benefit. Maintaining the appearance of self-importance* requires the expenditure of personal energy, lots of it. It takes a tremendous effort, even if it is unconscious, to keep up a façade that is, in the end, artificial. Most of us have been conditioned from very early on to do just this, with the result that we have been exhausting our precious energy for virtually our entire lives. The truth about this dynamic is perfectly logical when we understand that the self to whom self-importance is applied is ultimately not real. All one's thoughts of superiority and self-definition are really doing is causing resistance to the potential that is always present for a more joyful and fulfilling life experience to become manifest.

When you turn your attention to the practice of humility, you begin to reclaim lost energy, and paradoxically (or so it seems), become more effective during your daily routine. Others may see you as being

---

\* Self-importance is more than just an assumption of inherent superiority. Some teachers, Carlos Casteneda (3) and Eckhart Tolle (29), for instance, apply the concept of self-importance much more broadly. In this light, self-importance equates to one's preoccupation with self-definition in its entirety (likes, dislikes, beliefs, talents, personal history, physical characteristics, and even name) to the exclusion of what is Real about the Self. This preoccupation, or dream of the ego, is the primary cause of an individual's depletion of personal energy and subsequent suffering, the releasing of which, would allow the expansion of consciousness and transformation. Casteneda describes the powerful techniques of Don Juan for reclaiming lost energy, such as the practices of Stalking and Recapitulation. Victor Sanchez (38) catalogues all of these techniques from Castenda's books in *The Teachings of Don Carlos.*

more passive or mistake your lack of ego for lack of initiative. Rather than being less capable, you will become more efficient as you find more than enough energy to address the tasks that really need your involvement and the wisdom to let go of those that do not serve you. It may be that you have decided not to compete with someone else for attention, preferring instead to let them have the spotlight rather than force a negative situation that has no spiritual upside. Being humble means saying good-bye to misplaced responsibility. It means having more energy, being able to focus it in the right places, and at the same time, remembering to honor everyone, no matter what particular path they seem to be following. With this perspective, having humility is ultimately an advantage and a highly intelligent form of expression.

- *Acceptance*
Eckhart Tolle (29) calls this surrender, Raj (40) calls it choosing to set aside one's will, and other teachers have given it other names. I think of acceptance as forgiveness in real-time, that is, in the Now. If you allow that the present moment is all there really is (see The Bigger Picture in Chapter 6,), then *what is so* is *what is so*, and cannot be anything else. If you look closely at this moment *Right Now*, the fact is that we can do nothing about it. It is not possible to change it in the instant it is happening, and therefore, the only suitable position toward it is, indeed, acceptance.

You may say, "Well, what's going on in this moment is horrible, and I simply cannot accept it. I must do something, anything, rather than just sit passively with a vacant smile and make believe everything is all right." Perfectly understandable, considering the current conception of reality that we all share. At the same time, this is one very important place where the so-called rubber meets the road and where the opportunity exists to Feel Your Emotions (see above) in the moment. Also, like Forgiveness, above, it is possible for you to acknowledge your emotions, face them fully, and move through them, only now you will be doing it in the present, as events are actually happening. Yes, this may be difficult, but to whatever extent you can avoid habitual, knee-jerk reactions and remember to step back and observe first, you will gain an even greater magnitude of clarity and insight. "Remember to respond, not react." (40) Trust in this practice, and know that even a little acceptance goes a long way.

- *Equanimity*
Equanimity is similar to acceptance, but with the subtle, added dimension of Knowing. It could be said that with the greater acceptance of *what is so* comes the inner recognition that everything is as it should be, completely

> Practicing equanimity lets you become more of an observer of the Universe, curious to see how it will address your needs and desires.

appropriate to the current needs of each individual person and collective entity, whether it is a family, a business, or a country (5,15). This is one way to grasp the meaning of the phrases, "Let go and let God" and "Thy Will Be Done."

But, aren't these notions of surrender inconsistent with the inviolate permanence of each individual's free will that all spiritual masters repeatedly emphasize? Without the exercise of free will, what would happen to the personal control an individual requires in the world? The answer depends on who you think you really are. If you think you consist of only a body, along with the ego level of awareness that produces the experience most of us have, then you will perceive personal control as mandatory. Giving it up would seem to be akin to unilaterally disarming in the face of an advancing army, or, in a word, insane.

If you are really more, however, then perhaps will at the level of the ego is not the whole story. If, indeed, you really do have a soul, and this soul is your infinite, divine, and essential Being (34), would it not make sense that it holds your very best interests in the absolute highest regard? Would it not stand to reason that your soul sees a much larger territory than the "you" that you think you are, including your relationships to all the other people and events in your life? With this perspective, the practice of equanimity lets you begin to loosen your grip on personal control and become more of an observer of the Universe, curious to see how it will address your needs and desires. Eventually, it will dawn on you that God can configure your reality for a more salutary experience much better than you can, and paradoxically, you will become more relaxed as you learn to stop resisting this gift. In the end, "the only right use of will is to choose not to use it." (40)

- *Reverence*
We often consider reverence synonymous with great respect. When you respect others, you might admire something about them, possibly their accomplishments, determination, or intellect. And, in a larger sense, you could recognize and support their basic right to religious beliefs and cultural practices, even if they are unlike yours or are outside the norms of society. The American way of life is built on the idea that people from disparate backgrounds can live together peacefully and join cooperatively for the common good, essentially through the observance of respect for one another's differences.

Respect implies honoring the features of another's

life, or admiring, perhaps even fearing, their personal characteristics. Yet, all of these things are actually transient attributes of the person for whom we elicit the respect. If any of the attributes changed to a large enough degree, it's entirely possible that loathing would quickly replace respect, for instance. An example may be one who the community had held in high esteem as a model parent, but upon getting divorced, faces opprobrium for bringing upheaval and anguish to his or her family.

Reverence, on the other hand, comes from the deeper level of Being. Once you know the Truth about who you really are, it follows that you will know the Truth about everyone and everything else. Gary Zukav (34), in his commentary on this profound aspect of spiritual growth, makes clear that, "Reverence is engaging in a form and depth of contact with Life well beyond the shell of form and into essence." Little by little, you begin to relate to the eternal being that is a fundamental part of each and every thing (29), looking beyond the superficial layer of ego or form that may be presenting itself to you. As you do this, it becomes more and more difficult to inflict violence on another being, including the apparently inconsequential. When they say, "He wouldn't hurt a fly" about you, they will not realize how accurate that statement literally is. If you do swat a fly, as one who practices reverence, you will do it with forethought, weighing whether a valid reason exists to do it and how you will feel if you do it. Zukav sums it up well: "The decision to become a reverent person is essentially the decision to become a spiritual person."

- *Detachment*
  As your conscious awareness expands and a sense of internal calm takes root, you will find yourself being less reactive than before in emotionally charged relationships

and situations. Your feelings will change for a period of time and seem unfamiliar. You may find yourself wondering why you don't seem to care as much anymore. Guilt may even rear its ugly head. After all, aren't indifference, apathy, aloofness, unconcern,

> You do not practice detachment. You practice not turning away from it when it comes.

and coldness all synonyms for detachment? Yes, but a thesaurus doesn't take into account the subtle, but fundamental, distinctions necessary when we use detachment in a spiritual context (27).

What has actually happened is that the ego's hold on you has begun to diminish, with the automatic effect that the energy behind negative forms of expression is less available. Up until this point, you may have believed that many of these behaviors were demonstrable proof of concern or love (29). Perhaps you and your significant other had always argued frequently, a pattern you both accepted as a normal display of caring. When you arrive at the point of knowing that the arguing was really about possessiveness, neediness, or mistrust and you stop doing it, the relationship must change in some way. It's unlikely that you will go back to the bickering once you have experienced the alternative, but if your partner is not able to understand, the adjustment could be uncomfortable. You do not practice detachment. You practice not turning away from it when it comes, understanding that detachment is part and parcel of one's spiritual evolution.

Let me close this section with some personal remarks. I suspect that some people I know would look at me right now and judge me as not being exemplary in many of these expressions of Love. And, if that is the case, in this respect, I understand their perception. Certainly, I am not at the point where I am forgiving, grateful, or humble all of the time. I still get impatient, act ignorantly, and have my attachments as everyone else does. As I have said, I know that mastery is not yet within my grasp. Frankly, it's sobering to realize how much I have raised the bar for myself by writing openly about these subjects.

Still, others do not see my inner landscape. They aren't aware of what my intent is in spite of appearances. In keeping with the discussion of Humility above, it has become easier for me to release the need to convince other people about the rightness of a position I have taken, even though it certainly would make it easier for me at times. This may be construed as uncaring or unintelligent behavior on my part, when it's not understood that I am actually making a conscious decision to exercise nondefensiveness instead.

Although I am still influenced by the pull of cultural expectations, as most people are, to an increasing degree, I try to rely on my internal sense of Integrity for the answer to what is appropriate. To my chagrin, I find this often places me at odds with collective perceptions and judgments. Yet, it's a relief to know that I am where I am, at my "leading edge."* Everyone who is not yet awake has one, and no two are the same. I start from wherever that may be in any given moment. At the bottom line, it only matters that I recognize I am completely responsible for my thoughts, words, and deeds, and for whether I have done my best. Only I can know that.

---

\* This is a term from Raj (40) to indicate that each individual is always encountering his or her most ideal conditions for spiritual growth, regardless of appearances.

# Chapter 6

## The Bigger Picture

God is an intelligible sphere—a sphere known
to the mind, not to the senses—whose center is
everywhere and whose circumference is nowhere.
And the center … is right where you're sitting.
And the other one is right where I'm sitting.

*—Joseph Campbell*

The Messiah will come only when he is no longer
necessary; he will come only on the day after his
arrival.           *—Franz Kafka*

There are always those who take it upon themselves
to defend God, as if Ultimate Reality, as if the
sustaining frame of existence, were something
weak and helpless.   *—From the novel, Life of Pi.*

Who is qualified to speak of life's mysteries on a grand scale?
Recognized experts in their fields? Scientists? Religious leaders?
How about philosophers? People in a particular discipline devote
a great deal of time searching for the truth, or at least as clear
an understanding of reality as can be determined. The pursuit
of knowledge is noble and has always been part of what drives
us as human beings. However, as we accumulate and interpret

Craig Bruce

knowledge within a discipline, our knowledge inherently relies on an increasingly ingrained set of rules and processes about how to define and categorize reality. This is not necessarily a negative thing, in and of itself. It's just that too often the respective disciples become highly identified with their rules and processes to the point where their perceptions become beliefs, usually excluding all the others' perceptions as automatically invalid.

This identification can be due not only to fervent belief, but also to self-serving or fear-based motivations, among them the urge to further or defend one's social standing or power. Historical examples of the tendency of science and religion to resist unsanctioned beliefs abound. One of the best known was the philosophical uproar caused by Copernicus's theory

> It may seem inconsistent to say that perception of a God-given, universal truth can change; but, as your awareness expands, indeed it can.

that the earth revolved around the sun, that the universe was not geocentric, and the implied consequence that man's godlike status did not necessarily grant him superiority to the rest of nature. As the philosopher William James once observed, "A new idea is first condemned as ridiculous and then dismissed as trivial, until finally, it becomes what everybody knows."

Underneath all the competing beliefs about reality is ... Reality, on which no single person or system of thought actually has a monopoly. Each discipline certainly has a valuable role to play in helping humanity to peel back the infinite layers of the universal onion. Science, religion, and philosophy, when practiced with integrity have obviously contributed greatly to the higher good of humanity. But, ultimately, the only arbiter of the Truth is the individual, who takes in information—scientific, religious, or otherwise—and then has unique experiences that combine with the information to form a singular view of Reality. All of the singular views contribute to the various common views humans have—family, work, country, even science and religion—and these are fed back into each individual view in a never-ending cycle of changing perception.

Moreover, Reality is ultimately beyond intellectual understanding. The scientist's towering intellect can still only address and classify an infinitesimally small portion of what there is to Know. Reality beyond the world of three dimensions is ultimately unknowable to the three-dimensional mind. The most sophisticated theories and experiments are only descriptions of the real article and can only point us in the direction of the Truth. The essence of Life will never be reduced to a set of formulas. Just consider the miraculous, cosmic intelligence that must be present to make possible the most mundane and taken-for-granted things—the instantaneous construction of a coherent sentence in the proper context as it is being spoken, for instance.

Similarly, the religious leader's unshakable beliefs are based largely on the ideas and customs of ancient cultures long gone. Perhaps we were always meant to change our beliefs as the centuries passed and as our field of vision expanded. The most sincere words and thoughts only point to the experiences they represent. So, to answer the question of who is qualified to talk about Universal Truth, we all are. It is only necessary to remain open to new, meaningful information that may not be consistent with the systems of thought from our childhood or current frames of reference and to approach our personal quest with as high a level of integrity as possible.*

In the spirit of encouraging this open-ended approach to Truth, I felt it would be helpful to briefly explain the essence of what I have come to understand about Reality, for two reasons. One is to whet your appetite to explore the experiential wisdom that has existed for thousands of years and is now available to you. Perhaps a fresh, new way of seeing this "sustaining frame

---

*   *The Marriage of Sense and Soul* by Ken Wilber (22) is a thorough and lucid argument that the world has reached a point where it must unite "valid science" and "valid religion," while discarding "bogus" theological and scientific dogmas.

of existence" can serve to help you question whether there isn't more to everything than you thought and to ask, "How can I start to see the 'more of everything' for myself?"

My second purpose is to cast these basic principles in bold relief against the traditional, but limited, beliefs we have always depended on for guidance. As I have said before, this challenge is daunting, first, because we have a long-standing identification with our beliefs, and second, because the Truth can initially appear to be a maddening riddle when it is expressed in words. There is just no way, for instance, to rationalize how God has always been or to conceptualize a fourth spatial dimension in a mind with three-dimensional awareness. Still, while pondering these concepts is not the same as the direct experience of them, the act of orienting yourself mentally will ground you for the encounters to come. Once experienced, these principles become self-evident, and then the words suddenly become illuminated with meaning. The intellect certainly can be a wonderful enabler of spiritual evolution, just not in the overwhelmingly dominant position we have accorded it in our traditional disciplines of inquiry.

Your sense of the truth will also change as your understanding deepens, just as people several centuries ago finally realized that the earth is round, and just as we now are finding that planets do in fact revolve around other stars besides the Sun. It may seem inconsistent to say that perception of a God-given, universal truth can change, but as your awareness expands beyond three dimensions and a fixed sense of linear time, indeed it can. The same goes for manmade concepts of right and wrong. In the past, it was a moral imperative to burn witches at the stake for being agents of the devil, but we left behind that primitive obligation long ago. In our culture today, we often use a virtual stake with the aim of excluding certain groups of people who don't follow conventions. This too, will change.

That's why, if you accept that "there is something I do not know, the knowing of which could change everything," there is no point in continuing to hold onto rigid beliefs or adhering to years of cultural conditioning in its numerous forms. It takes patience, persistence, faith, and, sometimes, courage to open up to what you ultimately will find makes perfect sense. Here, then, simply stated, are the basic, life-affirming principles that govern our existence (5,11,24,29,40).

## God Is Love

The fundamental energy of the Universe that underlies everything seen and unseen is Love. This is not the multifaceted human emotion usually associated with the word love. No, this is the infinite Life Force that is felt as unfathomable peace and joy when it is beheld. While Love cannot be conceived by the human mind, the human who is being in the present moment will experience it. The experience of it is not dependent on any other person or thing. It is unconditional, completely free, always present, and without limit. Divine Love has no opposite. In an absolute sense, Love is all there is.

Every element of matter in existence has, at its core, this essence of Life. Everything is alive, even the chair you are perhaps sitting on. Consider that the particles making up an atom are arrayed in a proportion roughly the same as the solar system. The illusion of solidity is maintained only by the electrons (planets) whizzing around the nucleus (sun) at hundreds of miles per second.[7] What seems to us to be a tangible world is really illusory, consisting of vast reaches of emptiness that dwarf the particles themselves.

Electrons really behave both as particles and waves, impossible to identify with any degree of certainty at any given time, their approximate location a matter of probability. Subatomic particles are constantly moving and vibrating, exhibiting the characteristics of either matter or energy, depending on how they are observed.[8] What seems to us to be a stable world is really ephemeral, consisting of matter that arises from, and returns to, the realm of energy.

What, then, *is* in the emptiness between the electrons and

the nucleus of an atom, or between the illusory electron clouds of multiple atoms, or between the stars and galaxies? Divine Love, Universal Intelligence, God. It's within and around all that is, and *it's the only thing that truly exists.*

## God Is Being

God did not create the Universe, step back, somehow outside of it, and then decide where each star or tree would be, or judge who should live and who should die. God *is* the Universe right now, a Divine process creating Itself anew in every moment, never knowing what will unfold next. In absolute Reality, unknowable and beyond all human imagining, the relative does not exist, with only total and utter perfection being possible. To know Itself

> God's infinite expressions of Creation are endowed with their own spontaneous creativity and sense of Being, so that God may know experientially the full extent of Itself.

experientially, the Divine continually manifests infinitely, moment by moment, within a limitless multitude of realities, in what we call the Universe.

God is Being only in the present moment, the eternal Now. In actuality, there is no past and no future. These are imaginings of the human ego that obscure the Now, the only place where the experience of Love is possible. While only Love in the Now is Real, fear in its many forms is what we perceive within our imagined past and future. Guilt, anger, drama, and self-importance are all entertained in a past being remembered right now, covering up the present moment. Similarly, worry and anxiety reside within a nonexistent, anticipated future that hasn't happened yet. Only the experience of God being in the Now is Real. Fear, existing only in an illusory past and future, each being imagined in the Now, is a dream.

Time, inexorably moving in a linear fashion from the past into the future, never really dwelling in the present, seems to be an immutable fact. Accepting that time is actually an illusion becomes easier when you reckon that, even in three dimensions, it is only a convention that depends upon human perception. Our agreed-upon sense of time—minutes, days, months—is one that has become ingrained in our experience from watching the motions of the sun, moon, and stars across the millennia. Still, every so often we do notice perception's effect on the notion of time. We have all heard the familiar statement about an athlete, a basketball player for instance, being in the zone, becoming unconscious, sinking shot after shot. That athlete will usually say later that time seemed to slow down, and the basket looked as big as a house. Indeed, even though only one game clock was ticking away the same seconds for all the players, the difference in the perception of one player was the factor that materially affected everyone's experience.

When we leave the familiar scale of our earthly existence, the relativity of time becomes more pronounced. In one well-known illustration, a person who leaves earth in a spaceship traveling near the speed of light will be years younger, upon returning, than the twin sibling he or she left behind. However, the traveler looking at a clock's minute hand while on the spaceship will perceive no difference from how fast it moved on earth before departing, and would swear that time had not changed at all. Yet, the fact is that time is relative, not fixed.[9] Actually, everything is occurring in the eternal Now and will be recognized as such when we see beyond deeply ingrained perceptual conventions.

**God Is One**
Everything is one thing, God. All of the infinite manifestations of Creation that appear to be separate are actually the Mind of God expressed, and the Mind of God is not divided within itself. The true state of being is Unity; separation is only an illusion manufactured by the human ego. Conversely, God is all there really is of any particular thing. God, being Universal Mind,

means that any particular thing actually exists as consciousness, regardless of the way we perceive it at any particular moment.

Our individual sovereignty, standing completely apart from any other entity or thing, is another attribute of existence that seems to be unyieldingly self-evident. But, while we are each endowed with individual and eternal self-consciousness as a natural consequence of Creation, we still do not exist outside of God. Our minds are part of the One Mind and, therefore, discrete boundaries do not really exist between us. Most of the time, our perception tells us that we are in separate physical bodies with minds somewhere inside our heads. Yet most of us have had some form of unitary experience—from knowing what another was going to say before he said it, to thinking about someone from long ago and seeing that person suddenly coming around the corner, to dreaming about a situation and having it materialize, to having the transcendent understanding of this Truth.

No object or information can travel faster than the speed of light in the universe, yet two particles separated by vast distances can affect each other's behavior instantaneously and predictably. Information is being shared between them that cannot be accounted for in physical terms.[10] What would be uniting them to be able to communicate outside of space and time? Universal Mind, the missing factor that is needed to explain communication at the speed of thought. Consciousness is specific and infinite at the same time, and someday, we will choose to directly experience both sides of this paradox for ourselves.

**God Is All There Is of Us**
Because God is perfect Love and God is the only thing going on, Humans are ultimately perfect, as well. The natural question, then, is how this can be so if we continually perceive imperfection, separation, and suffering? Why do we have to work, and why do poverty, disease, and war exist?

Simply put, God is all there is of us, or, in more traditional terms, each and every human being is made in God's image. This includes nothing less than the power to create our experience of Reality in any way we desire with complete free will. The truth is that we humans are much more than we realize, and this "much more" actually stands ready to express our never-ending, conscious experience, based on our individual and collective choices. God created the language, as it were, and we, not God, are responsible for the stories we author. A famous Bard once said, "All the world's a stage, And all the men and women merely players. They have their exits and their entrances; And one man in his time plays many parts ..." But, even more than this, we players are also simultaneously the playwrights and directors of our own creations.

For most of what we call recorded history, virtually all of us have chosen to remain unaware of our higher selves beyond the veil of beliefs, conventional wisdom, and cultural norms. For eons, we have collectively agreed to live within the duality, in its various forms, of right versus wrong, good versus evil, and moral versus immoral, when all along Love has been all that exists. Thoughts of fear entered our consciousness long ago, giving rise to the ego, persuading us to live within a tiny portion of Reality, constrained by self-imposed, artificial limitations. Our collective experience of suffering has been the natural effect of the decision to live in a small box. But, fear is not the opposite of Love, and fear is not real. There are no victims, not Really. We have freely made this perceptual choice, and we have the power to change it at any time we desire.

It may be, as Stanislav Grof describes in *The Cosmic Game* (6), that when all is said and done, two opposing divine forces govern Reality and the human being's role in its continual unfolding. One is the Divine's need to know Itself in ways that are not possible in the pure state of Absolute Perfection. This state is a singularity, in which there are no opposites, and therefore no frame of reference by which this perfection can be compared and experienced. In the realm of the Absolute, where no duality exists, it is possible to contemplate the concept of hot and cold, for instance, but no avenue by which to have the manifest knowledge of the infinite expression of temperature. Indeed, the term "cosmic boredom" was coined to capture the essence of this Divine conundrum.

To solve this problem, Absolute Consciousness in an act of supreme Creation individuated itself into countless realms and units of Being, that together comprise All That Is. These infinite expressions of Creation, while still part of the Absolute Mind, are endowed with their own creativity and sense of Being, and the continual interplay between them provides endless cosmic adventures where the full extent of All That Is can be known. The special role that religions ascribe to Human Beings in God's Plan is really one of carrying out the essential purpose God has to know Itself fully.

However, for this "cosmic game" to have meaning, the many planes of reality, which are fundamentally illusions, must appear absolutely real. The individual units of consciousness must forget where they came from and lose themselves in the game. And, here is where the second and opposing cosmic force enters the picture. At the core of every one of God's individuations, the certain, if veiled, knowledge of its pure Divinity and spiritual nature exists. For this reason, the inherent desire exists in all of the infinite units of consciousness to return to and merge with their Source. Grof writes, "In essence, we do not have a fixed identity and can experience ourselves as anything on the continuum between the embodied self and Absolute Consciousness. ...Since by our true nature we are unlimited spiritual beings, we enter the cosmic game on the basis of a free decision and get trapped by the perfection with which it is executed."

> At the core of every one of God's creations, the certain, if veiled, knowledge of its pure Divinity and spiritual nature exists.

While most of us are not yet aware of our perfection, we are very familiar with a continuous, moment-to-moment sense of self-identity. This individual sense of continuity will never leave us during our life, a single Life that is eternal with no beginning or end, consisting of infinite conscious experiences, including what we think of as birth and death. In fact, we never lose the thread of our consciousness, regardless of physical appearances. It's just that, for most of us, our current experience of duality in the physical world is so compelling that it masks the more of everything that there is for us to see. As Grof indicates, the truth that "we are not human beings having a spiritual experience, we are spiritual beings having a human experience" has been forgotten. There is no death. The act of reestablishing this natural frame of reference and moving beyond "the taboo against knowing who you are," is what is known as waking up.

## God Is Beyond Our Best Concepts

In the beginning … humans lived among the grand panorama of nature, trying to understand its meaning and their relationship to it. A few of their number had revelatory encounters of All That Is that transcended the physical reality they had known and gave to them a direct experience of the infinite Peace and Love of the Universe. They tried to communicate to the others what they had discovered using words the best they could. They told them that these discoveries were available to anyone who came to them with pure intent. In most cases, however, the others regarded these individuals as prophets and masters, and many of the others began to worship them and become their followers.

The words the masters spoke about their divine experience were recorded into great texts, at first capturing very well the message of Spirit's unending Love. As time went on and the masters departed, other leaders appeared who built structures around this core wisdom, including laws, rituals, and beliefs according to the cultural biases of the times. These structures gradually coalesced into a doctrine of faith. Eventually, it became a requirement to follow the doctrine to receive God's love and mercy, and by extension, the acceptance of the others in the faith. Over the centuries, each faith's view of reality came to be seen by most of its adherents as the best, and sometimes, the only singularly true view.

According to this brief history of the world, all religious doctrines, whatever their individual differences, have become removed from the fundamental nature of the Universe. This is evident in our respective rites of worship, much of which are spent lavishing praise on the Almighty, or asking Him (not Her, or It) to forgive us for our weaknesses and transgressions. The error in this thinking is that it places humanity, and everything else, in a position that is separate from God and portrays God as responsible for our creations.

Stop for a moment and imagine what would happen if everyone understood that each of us really does have the power of creation, that every thought, word, and deed of ours has tangible consequences. And, imagine a world where people acted as though they truly had a connection to, and therefore,

> Hidden within traditional religious observance, we can still find the direct, undistorted nature of spiritual experience.

an impact on, each other and the earth. Would the quality of physical existence be better served by this approach or by praying to a being we are supposedly not part of to save us from ourselves? Would it not be a better world if we actually considered the very real effect we each have as individuals on our collective experience? Once more, the answer becomes evident when you go within.

Religious observance today may largely obscure the direct experience of what is essentially beyond words, yet it is still evident, to some degree, in undistorted form, contained in very familiar services and ceremonies. Consider the following three passages from a Sabbath prayer book followed by some Reform Jewish congregations.[11]

> *"A time can come to us when our hearts are filled*
> *with awe: suddenly the noise of life will be stilled,*

*as our eyes open to a world just beyond the border of
our minds. All at once there is a glory in our souls!
The Holy God! O majestic Presence! O world ablaze
with splendor!"*

Or,

*"Therefore, O God, when doubt troubles us, when
anxiety makes us tremble, and pain clouds the mind,
we look inward for the answer to our prayers. There
may we find you ... "*

Or,

*"And it has been written: 'Fire shall be kept burning
upon the altar continually, it shall not go out.' Our
heart is the altar. In every occupation let a spark of
the holy fire remain within you, and fan it into a
flame."*

Captured beautifully, right there under our noses every week, is
the basic nature of spiritual experience. Indeed, the first passage
describes as well as any the encounter with one's Soul, an encounter
completely in the present moment, revealing an all-encompassing
realm that surpasses beliefs and words. The second illuminates
what prayer truly is, going within and listening. That's where we
find the answers to the mysteries of life. In the third, we are being
reminded that our true Being is eternal and that we can become
conscious of this fact at any time by turning our attention in
this direction. Of course, by not actually going within, beyond
the ego, the words will remain just words to become identified
with, and they will have no real meaning. But, having established
subjective knowledge of these passages, which has an impact far
beyond the conceptual, it becomes incomprehensible that a set
of beliefs—convictions about life, but not actually Life itself—
would reveal the Truth to anyone.

Even if you haven't yet discovered this intuitively, consider a logical approach to the question of whether anyone, by virtue of his or her religious (or scientific) beliefs, has an inherent claim to the truth or is exclusively entitled to God's favor. At root, there are three fundamental views of human existence. The first says that we live a singular life on earth as purely biological beings in a material reality governed by random events. We eventually die and cease to exist. In this scenario, how can anyone know the truth if nothing has any meaning? We do have an established process of objective inquiry known as the scientific method. But, ultimately, that can only guide us to the "how," not the "why," of things. If "why"—that is, Meaning—is not somehow part of the discovery equation, then everything simply becomes a question of "engineering." Nothing really has any inherent purpose or makes any difference.*

---

* I understand the atheist's rejoinder: "The hard truth is that 'why' simply does not exist. No one can objectively demonstrate the Meaning that supposedly is there, waiting to be discovered." Ken Wilber, Stanislav Grof, and others, have articulated what I believe to be a cogent counterargument. While internal subjective knowing cannot be proven or communicated by objective means, it can still be shared with others in a scientific manner. A highly sophisticated body of spiritual knowledge has, in fact, been developed by a multitude of cultures over thousands of years through their collective research, experimentation, publication, and peer review. True, there were no modern scientific journals or practitioners with advanced academic credentials. But, over a long period, individuals in these cultures tried many techniques to expand consciousness in countless experiments. They compared and evaluated their results, and then sanctioned only the techniques agreed to be most effective. The outcome of all of this research is what Grof refers to as the "technology of the sacred." This technology, although not manifested in physical form, does provide time-tested, reliable, and repeatable methods by which Meaning may be experienced and disclosed. But, this empirical verification will happen only if the individual—atheist, agnostic, or religious believer—is willing

The second view says that we each lead a singular life and then proceed to a different plane of existence forever. Obviously, there are many variations on this theme, but most have in common a God who sits in judgment of us, deciding our fate. Most say He decides whether our eternal existence will be heavenly or hellish. Regarding this view, as well, how can anyone claim that his or her beliefs are the truth? Here, no one existed prior to his birth and no one could have chosen his life circumstances, so much of which determines beliefs and attitudes. If someone is Hindu or Catholic, or, for that matter, African or Swedish, and you regard any of these as incorrect or undesirable, what choice did he or she have in the matter? Similarly, if someone is born into great wealth

---

to employ it consistently with an open mind. Wilber reinforces these points by reminding us that logic and mathematics are also nonphysical constructs of the mind that are experienced subjectively by the individual. Nonetheless, they are still shared to provide the collective basis for our science and technology, and all of the physical laws and structures they engender.

What about the argument that, even if mystical experience exists, it's really just another of the brain's biological processes? This position suggests that there is actually nothing "spiritual" going on; only a set of neurons causing physical sensations that science will eventually isolate and document. The same can be said of the mind in general, and any of its contents. Perhaps. However, as Grof points out, this premise is a matter of conjecture, albeit one that does carry ample weight in our materially oriented culture. A better view, I believe, is illustrated by a Grof analogy. Saying that the brain and the mind are equivalent is like saying that a television set and the show you are watching "on" TV are one in the same. They are not. The show (mind) is electromagnetic energy that originates from a distant source and has no form or boundary. This amorphous energy is actually being rendered locally by the television (brain) as something that can be physically understood. The mind really does not exist within the brain, even though it may feel that way to most people.

and his life benefits materially from this fact, did that person have any control in setting it up this way?

If we agree that the life circumstances we are born into shouldn't make anyone's views or worth greater or lesser, then we are left with the deeds we do during our life in the circumstances we happen to encounter. Here is where most religious doctrine says God's judgment comes into play, and they are clear that judgment is reserved for God only. The question is whose set of rules is correct concerning what is needed to withstand God's scrutiny of our deeds? If you say, "My religion is correct," what about the rest of us who weren't fortunate enough to have been born into your religion with the right set of rules? Is the requirement that you must surrender yourself to the one and only savior, or is it that you must be one of the chosen people, or that you must pray a certain number of times per day facing in a certain direction? Clearly, if the opportunity for salvation is determined in this way, either by chance or by divine will, then most of humanity wouldn't have much hope. Sure, all one has to do to be saved is to adopt the so-called correct way of thinking, but as we know, a person's background, heavily influenced by the very circumstances he or she was born into, will usually conspire against this act.

An honest appraisal of the second view of existence leads to the conclusion that there is a substantial risk of insularity and, by extension, easily justified abuse against other human beings, although most of the world continues to operate under some version of this approach. And, if we think about it, two basic orientations to conventional religious practice exist, one of which has come to the fore only in recent times. The first is the traditional one where people really are trying to be virtuous through the expression of their religion's doctrine. Here, the believers, in general, can be said to be sincerely honoring their integrity by trying to act from a larger frame of reference. If one is truly embodying his or her beliefs in terms of the foundational

Love that is at the core of all religions, then this is simply another of the many paths that lead to awakening.

The problems begin when one moves beyond the practice of Love into the realm of doctrine, and the beliefs become laden with requirements and conditions. This naturally leads to sanctions and punishments, and ultimately, to the perpetuation of fear and guilt. Love tends to get left behind in this scenario. Taken to the extreme, we have seen repeatedly from our history that an overly fervent conviction in what is considered to be godly has led to the torture and death of countless people who had a different set of ideas. Much of this misery was exacerbated by empires through the ages that found fear-based religious doctrines to be highly useful in furthering the expansion of their power and wealth. This continues today.

The second orientation to conventional religion is subtler and parallels the accelerating complexity in today's world, especially in the United States. To a greater extent, it seems that more people identify with their religion for what can be termed cultural reasons. Being guided by doctrine is no longer the primary aspiration of religious affiliation. For many, their faith has become a part of a cultural identity that includes other facets of life, such as economic class, social status, ethnicity, or even political party membership. In the highly artificial environment we have collectively built, the exterior aspects of reality have become the primary barometer of worth, and religion is just another of these. A sincere quest to understand the nature of the universe has been crowded out by the distraction of an empty façade.

A third way of looking at our existence is that we are really spiritual beings and that we eternally manifest in different physical forms for the purpose of spiritual evolution and learning. In this approach, too, many variants are possible. The best known of these includes the Eastern concepts of reincarnation and karma. In this instance, we continually return to earth in different form to work off our karmic debt. Negative deeds naturally lead to the consequence of our having to experience the same conditions we imposed on others. As we go through this learning process over many lives, our preoccupation with illusion diminishes. Eventually, we reach a level of spiritual mastery and move on to other forms of existence.

The historically esoteric views of eternal spiritual evolution that are now coming into our awareness add the ideas that we are much more multidimensional than even reincarnation implies, and that our many incarnations and dimensional instances really exist at once. That is, all existence is actually in the timeless, eternal moment of Now, and the past and future are really illusions created by the ego within the domain of physical reality. The higher levels of our being (i.e., the Soul) have the full picture of all of our various individual manifestations. We choose each of our individual experiences in physical reality prior to incarnating to create opportunities for remembering Who we truly are, thereby serving the continuing spiritual evolution of the Soul. However, this experiential template is not cast in stone, as conventional notions of reincarnation would indicate, and can be changed at any time through the awakening of conscious awareness during our time on earth. This has also been called dying before you die, or relinquishing your self-definition and seeing the bigger picture right here, right now.

> The person you are observing is walking a spiritual path not known to you, one that is much greater in scope than any of his or her current superficial characteristics would indicate.

The model of humans as multidimensional spiritual beings suggests even more strongly that religious superiority is a completely erroneous assumption. If we are infinite, eternal beings, our current earthly incarnation is but one of many. We may be a certain religion, race, or have a certain economic status in this time and place, but what we think we are superior to, we actually have been or will be in other earthly experiences.

And, each of these incarnations, including their main features and conditions, we have brought to ourselves to allow the totality of experience to become ours and God's. The attribute of religion is only one of the props we use to play our current roles that may lead us at any time to spiritual awakening. When you look at another person who is different from you and consider this idea, all thoughts of superiority must necessarily recede. The person you are observing is walking a spiritual path not known to you, one that is much greater in scope than any of his or her current superficial characteristics would indicate.

Theologies that promote the sharing of Love between its followers are a blessing. The rituals we have known all of our lives provide meaning during our times of celebration, and comfort us through times of trial. But, those that encourage a position of inherent superiority, or the conditional withholding of God's Love, engender guilt and fear. These assumptions are insidiously polarizing and cause us to waste vast amounts of our precious energy in a pursuit that ultimately has no value for any group. Restoring the search for Spirit and the *direct experience* of It to an elevated place in our religions' raison d'être is vitally important. Mainstream religion, in the absence of its original experiential bond with the Love of Spirit, has lost its way.

Many have now come to this conclusion. They have decided to remove the layers of religious doctrine and return to the basic search for Truth, looking as much within as without. When they do look to external wisdom, they are less inclined to shut out ideas just because they happen to cross the boundaries of belief sanctioned by a particular faith. Their litmus test is an internal one whose only requirement is the presence of Integrity and Love. As this shift in consciousness gathers momentum, the result will be welcome news to a world critically in need of healing.

### Toward Seeing the Bigger Picture

In considering these spiritual principles that govern our reality, the possibility that a vast unknown but knowable domain of direct experience is waiting to be embraced may be planted in your mind. It suddenly may seem more reasonable to actually become curious enough, in spite of lifelong habits and conditioning, to earnestly investigate this domain. Once you do this, and begin to replace old beliefs with new understandings, you will eventually establish a much bigger frame of reference in which you view your life and the world at large.

> Being precedes doing or having. You are happy because this is whom you have chosen to be; events and circumstances follow in kind. Your Being, the real You, is eternal and invulnerable.

Consider an analogy that may help better explain this point. Imagine that your entire existence can be spread out across the surface of a huge field. Suppose one of the major aspects of your life at this time is your job. Perhaps you have built a highly successful career and, consciously or not, you now believe this to be a key part of your identity. Your position affords you a certain lifestyle and level of status that society recognizes as special, and you (your ego, really) have come to depend on this specialness, equating it with self-worth. Suddenly, you lose your job. Now, imagine that on the field where your entire existence is spread before you, the event of losing your job actually covers a very tiny area in comparison to all the events that comprise the whole.

How you perceive this one event, and its relationship to your state of being, has everything to do with your perspective. If you are hovering ten feet above the field and can only see the loss of your job and the surrounding circumstances of your immediate life situation, your reaction may be concern, depression, or even panic. If your position above the field is elevated to one hundred feet, you may see five years of your current life before you and realize that the loss of this job ended up leading to opportunities you couldn't have possibly been aware of at ten feet. Now at one thousand feet, your view encompasses the whole of your current life. Here you understand that, through this event, not only did other opportunities present themselves, but also grand lessons in life were learned, lessons that are priceless. Maybe you learned not to be angry, the value of patience, or how to forgive.

Then, at ten thousand feet, a truly amazing thing happens. You see past the boundaries of your current life, and it becomes clear that you take what you learn with you. There are more lives to live and more lessons to experience in more levels of reality, all of which are ultimately based on Love. Eternal Love is all there really is. When you glimpse this truth, you learn a lesson in eternity. Your state of being has nothing to do with external circumstances. Being precedes doing or having. Being happy, for instance, is not the result of *having* an important job or *making* a lot of money. You are happy because this is whom you have chosen to be; events and circumstances follow in kind. Your Being, the real You, is eternal and invulnerable.

Once you glimpse one of the higher perspectives, it becomes more difficult to go back down to ten feet and stay there. You may go down there occasionally, but now you know that the higher you go, the more Love there is, and that's what we naturally aspire to be. As this idea takes root, what you value in your current life changes dramatically. Yet most of us, at the ten-foot level, are operating within the prevailing views of our culture as our main frame of reference. If we are going to expand our field of vision, something the world now cries for, we need to honestly reexamine some of our cherished beliefs. We need to become openly curious to move beyond our usual definitions and sanctions to see what is really there. The bigger picture awaits us if only we will allow ourselves to see it.

# Chapter 7

## Experiential Guide
## —Meditation Program and Other Practices

If you do not go within, you go without.
> —*From Conversations with God, Book 1*

True intelligence operates silently. Stillness is where creativity and solutions to problems are found. —*Eckhart Tolle*

### A Beginning Meditation Program

The daily practice of meditation can be an essential part of any person's evolution to a more peaceful and relaxed state of mind. After some time, you will find that the relaxation carries over into your daily routine and that negative emotions no longer seem as powerful. You may think more clearly and be more alert. Your health may even improve.

> There is no *right* way to gain access to what is inherently yours. Just become still and allow whatever happens to happen.

It comes down to this: Your attention is a part of you that is very powerful, much more than you are normally aware. In most everyone's daily routine, attention is fragmented among many internal distractions of different kinds, whether they are anxieties, guilt, worry, or running mental movies about various dramas in our lives. The point is that incessant thinking, which is almost always present if you take the time to observe yourself, continually distracts your attention and keeps it unfocused. But, from what is your attention being distracted? You are distracting yourself from the experience of the real You.

Meditation is a very effective way to look inside yourself, to see the essence of who you really are, mainly by relaxing your body and moving your awareness away from thinking. Connecting with this Essence gives you a much different perspective on your life. You realize that there is more to life than only what you can think or experience through your five senses. Meditation makes it possible to access an intelligence that is not related to intellect or cognition. It is far more powerful and may be thought of as a knowing at a very deep level. All of this is a part of every human being and is available to anyone who cares to look. If you happen to be skeptical, try to set aside your preconceptions for a while. Approach this endeavor with curiosity, a sense of adventure, and the idea that you are doing something worthwhile for yourself.

- **Daily Schedule**
  To get results, adhere to a regular schedule and maintain it consistently. The initial goal is to become proficient at relaxing the body and clearing the mind of thought. Most thought is actually mental noise and is a detriment to your well-being. By becoming clear of thought, you allow yourself to be in the present moment, making room for insight and wholeness to enter.

  This may (or may not) be difficult at first. In any event, it doesn't mean that you should force yourself to *not* think to the point that it creates anxiety and stress. When thoughts enter the mind, as they usually will, just refocus on your meditation. Also, don't judge your thoughts in any way when they appear. *There are no requirements or measures of success.* Eventually, if you maintain your schedule, you will have conditioned yourself to reach a relaxed and clear state more easily.

- **Two Sessions per Day, Twenty Minutes Each**
  1. Morning session—Perform meditation in any position that allows comfort and relaxation. Do it sitting in a comfortable chair with the spine fairly erect or lying down. If you have responsibilities when you arise (children, pets), then a solution is to meditate as soon as you wake up while you are still in bed. No one will be aware that you are awake, so it will be possible to spend the next twenty minutes meditating. You can also awake twenty minutes earlier, if necessary. The additional benefit is that you will already be relaxed, because you have just been asleep for the night.
  2. Afternoon or evening session—A second daily session is helpful to reinforce the skills you are developing. Again, if you have family or other demands that prevent an afternoon session, one solution is to meditate when you are in bed and close your eyes for the night. Before falling asleep, you can take twenty minutes and, again, there will be no conflict with any other responsibilities. A possible benefit here is that you may fall asleep faster and have a much better night's rest.

- **Preparation for a Session**
  Quiet and comfort will help you make progress. If you do your meditation in the home, it should be in a room separate from other people with the door shut. A white noise machine is very beneficial, both to block out unwanted noise and to provide a consistent and predictable background. Room temperature should be normal—too hot or too cold may be distracting. There is no perfect or required position for meditating. The chair

or bed should be comfortable, but not so soft that it does not provide good support. Having said all this, don't get hung up on finding the perfect position or eliminating every possible distraction. Ultimately, you want to reach a point of being able to accept whatever conditions are present, although this may take some practice.

- **Meditation Process**
  There is no perfect way to meditate. It is a very personal experience, and this can be difficult to communicate verbally to another person. Many different styles and methods exist, but the steps below* are a good way to get started. After a while, you will want to add your own ideas, depending on what works best for you (see the next section below for thirteen recommended enhancements).
  1. Lying down or sitting, find a comfortable position. If lying down, a pillow behind the head and under the knees is suggested, although the head and knees should not be elevated too much. Once you are stationary, try to resist the urge to move. Gradually, you will forget about urges to reposition different parts of your body.
  2. To begin, close your eyes and take five deep breaths. Inhale slowly and fully, and then try to exhale even more slowly than you inhaled. When you inhale, bring the air into your belly first, and then let your chest expand to complete the breath.
  3. Now, go more deeply into a peaceful state by counting from one to twenty for five sets (i.e., you will have repeated counting to twenty in five cycles, for a total of one hundred counts). Count mentally, not verbally. As you count each number, visualize it in your mind.

---

\* As mentioned earlier, this process was influenced by many authors and sources including: Jose Silva, Eckhart Tolle, Paul Tuttle, Ken Wilber, et al.

Try to really see each number. It can look any way you want. As you count, it is very important to match the counting to the rhythm of your breathing. Time each count as you exhale. For instance, the pattern would be: <inhale><exhale & visualize #1>, <inhale><exhale & visualize #2>, and so on until you get to twenty. Then, start at one again and repeat this process until you have done five sets of twenty.

As you visualize the numbers, try to see the number in your third eye. This is the point between your eyes where your nose meets your forehead. With your eyes closed, you can "look through" this point to some distance in front of you. Try to imagine a distance of about six feet.

4. Now relax your body as completely as possible. You will be surprised at how much tension is present. Focus on your feet, and then imagine all the muscles going completely slack and all the tension completely disappearing. You can even visualize your feet turning into pure energy, no longer being physical at all. Repeat the same process in the lower legs, upper legs, back, abdomen, shoulders, arms, hands, neck, and face. Certain areas, such as the neck and face, can exhibit more tension and may take more time, but spending about a minute on each area is a good rule of thumb to start.

5. After meditating for a period of weeks or months, you will find that just doing steps 2, 3, and 4 will enhance your inner state to one of peacefulness. And, over time, you will find that is possible to go deeper. Once you are in this relaxed state, you may want to take a few minutes to do special visualizations or affirmations that reinforce, and ultimately manifest in your experience, your highest and grandest visions of what you aspire to be as a human being.

6. When you are finished meditating, return to an active state by counting backward from twenty to one, again,

visualizing each number as you exhale. As you count, gently wiggle your fingers and toes. Then, stretch slowly, and open your eyes.

## Thirteen Ways to Enrich Your Meditations

After you are satisfied with the process outlined above, you may want to reflect on any of these expanded perspectives while you are in the meditative state, to further experience That which you truly are. Allow whatever happens to happen.

- *"Who Am I?"*
  Begin by noticing the void you are in at the moment. Generally, it's black because your eyes are closed, although some intermittent visual images may be coming and going. Be with this void for a while, and then try to locate yourself, your consciousness, in the void. At first, it may seem to be just behind your eyes, and then you may let it move to other parts of your body. Once you have identified your consciousness, try to find the boundaries of it, and notice that you can't—there is no boundary to find. Finally, contemplate that perhaps this void is the true reality, not the one you will see again when you open your eyes. Let yourself settle into the stillness of this awareness, and allow it to take you deeper into the infinity within yourself.

- *"I Am No-Thing"*
  Start by mentally repeating, with each breath, "I Am Nothing." After a while, notice that what you are saying is not that you are nonexistent, or small. You are actually saying, "I Am No-Thing"—that is, you are not a thing, finite in its form and scope. You are infinite, boundless, beyond all form. Play with this idea for a while, and realize the difference between "Nothing" and "No-Thing." Then,

repeat this phrase: "All Is No-Thing," meaning that, just like you, the true state of everything is boundless.

- *"I Am Not My Body"*\*
  Entertain the idea that you have a physical body but that You are not actually your body. You are consciousness. Assume the perspective of the real You, consciousness, and then simply become an observer. Notice your body and how it resides within your mind, not the other way around. Observe your body—your lungs breathing, your heart beating, the blood flowing—and see how the You that is watching is not the lungs, heart, blood, and so on. Have no judgment or thought about what it is you observe, other than to feel love and gratitude for your body. Notice how much you appreciate how it tries to serve You while you have it.

- *"I Am Not My Mind"*
  Entertain the idea that you have thoughts, beliefs, and emotions, but that You are actually none of these. These thoughts, beliefs, and emotions may have seemed to have a life of their own, but now you will let them go for a while and discover what is buried underneath them. Focus on your third eye, the point between your eyes where your nose meets your forehead. Now watch that point for the next thought to appear. When it does, notice it, let go of it, and return your focus to your third eye. Don't labor over this process. You are merely an observer, watching your thoughts go by with no judgment or concern about what they are. As you do this, you will become aware of the spaces between the thoughts. Observe these spaces. What is there?

---

\* The "I Am Not My Body" and "I Am Not My Mind" meditations are similar to those suggested in Ken Wilber's book, *No Boundary* (25).

- *"I Am Listening to the Silence"*\*
  Entertain the idea that all sounds come from the silence and return there. The silence is more than just the absence of sound, and it has unlimited depth. Begin by noticing a sound, perhaps the roof creaking or the wind blowing through the trees outside your window. When that sound finishes, follow it back into the silence from where it originated, and stay there as long as you can. When you return from the silence, pick another sound, and follow it the same way. After doing this for a while, focus on the silence and its depth, not on the surface layer of sound. As you dwell in the silence, move your awareness into your body, and notice how still and peaceful your inner world is.

- *"I Am Relaxed to the Max"*
  You have just finished relaxing your body completely, or have you? Follow your breathing for a while, and then repeat the initial relaxation sequence. You may be surprised to find that as relaxed as you have become, some areas of your body, perhaps the thighs, shoulders, neck, or the area behind the eyes, can still be relaxed much more. You are now experiencing finer levels of body awareness than you knew existed. See the tension you were not previously aware of, and then let it go. Watch your body move into a delightful state of peacefulness, and observe your physical form change into the energy that it truly is.

- *"I See Beyond Myself"*
  Place your attention on your third eye, the point between the eyes where the nose meets your forehead. Then, look at a point beyond your third eye, perhaps to an imagined

---

\* The "I Am Listening to the Silence" meditation is based on Eckhart Tolle's teachings in his book, *The Power of Now* (29).

distance of a few feet. Become an impartial observer, watching for whatever may show up at any moment, but have no requirement or expectation that anything must show up. If thoughts or emotions come in, just let them pass, as you would watch someone walk by and disappear into the distance. Then, return your attention to the point beyond your third eye. What is there?

- *"I Am Everywhere"*
Through eons of going along unwittingly with prevailing mass perceptions, we believe that we are tiny physical bodies somewhere within a vast material universe. Consider the possibility that a larger experience is available to you if you dare to reach beyond collective beliefs and perceptual agreements. Begin to know the truth that you are much more than an amalgam of various forms of matter by inviting an experience of your body other than the one you automatically expect. As you lay in bed on your back, eyes closed in your deeply relaxed state, imagine that you are not actually in a horizontal position being held in place against the mattress by the force of gravity. Imagine, instead, that you are really laying with your back against the ceiling, firmly anchored to it by the equally powerful pull of magnetism. Picture the room in your mind from this vantage point. Deeply sense this reorientation within your body, and let in the expansion of your awareness that will come with it.

- *"I Have No Goal"*
Your entire life is usually an exercise in achieving, becoming, and measuring up to expectations. For now, you are going to drop all of these demands and just let yourself be as you are. Simply focus on your breathing, letting your inhales and exhales occur without any effort or direction. Just allow your lungs to fulfill their function,

and just observe. If thoughts or emotions come in, just let them pass, as you would watch someone walk by and disappear into the distance. Then return your attention to your breathing. Notice that there is no demand for you to do anything. You need do nothing. Just Be.

- *"I Am Perpetually Created Anew"*
  It may seem that everything remains virtually the same from one moment to the next. In reality, however, all things are infused with the Life Force of the Universe in each and every instant. This is the eternal process of Creation, and it includes you. The most easily seen parallel in the physical realm comes from an utterly awesome, but usually overlooked, source—the sun. Unimaginable amounts of energy spontaneously emanate from countless points of origin within the body of this miraculous entity. Just holding the vision, even for a moment, of the infinite, simultaneous, and overlapping instants of energy creation, bursting forth into being as heat and light, is enough to give anyone a visceral sense of reality beyond the limits of three dimensions. Like the sun, you have the Life Force of the Universe finding its way into the physical world in a perpetual flow from deep within. Go now into your body and sense this inexhaustible chain reaction of energy transformation. Feel the light that is being created, flowing out in waves from each and every point within you, endlessly, until you experience yourself as the sphere of Eternal, Divine Radiance that You truly are.

- *"I Love Myself"*
  Contemplate that you are already perfect. This is your natural state, covered up by erroneous beliefs about yourself accumulated with the passage of time. As you hold this idea, you may encounter anxious emotions,

feeling them in your gut, that seem to argue for your inherent guilt, lack of worth, or inadequacy. These emotions could be related to any number of issues, but the specifics are not important. Practice observing, in a detached manner, the anxiety at a physical level as it feels right now. Let judgments or thoughts about the underlying issues from the past slip by. Once you are simply being with the anxiety, move beyond it. Go within yourself, and find your inner child again, the part of you that has always been innocent and that you left behind over the years. Express your love for your inner child and your desire to reunite with it. Express your intent never to undervalue yourself again. Do not be surprised if a wonderful emotional release occurs.

- *"I Am Not My-self"*
  Creation is not something that occurred once a long time ago; it continues in a never-ending parade of change, moment by moment, forever. God, All That Is, or whatever you chose to call Universal Intelligence, is being spontaneously original in everything you experience, everywhere you look. Since you did not create yourself, and all of Creation is the manifestation of Divine will, you are literally an Idea in the Mind of God that is finding continual expression in the formation of reality. Therefore, the truth is that your mind and God's Mind are actually one. This fact terrifies your ego. The ego's defense, a grand illusion of separateness and individual authorship of thought and experience, is the reason that you have forgotten the truth of your universal perspective. After all, what would happen to the ego—the self (with a lowercase "s") you believe is real—if you were to

---

\* The "I Am Not My-self Meditation" is based on the teachings of Raj from the Northwest Foundation for "A Course in Miracles" (40).

acknowledge your true Identity? Dare to put the ego in its rightful, subordinate position, and access the Divine Truth of Who You Are by contemplating the profound meaning in any of these statements:

"I am a never-ending Idea in Your Mind."

"I am Being as You are Being Me."

"I am observing You Being Me."

Know that as you initially consider these statements, you may encounter significant discomfort or tension. After all, you are making a conscious decision, even if only for a few moments, to turn away from everything you have known and to "trust into the unknown."* However, taking a step forward when it's not obvious where your foot will land is sometimes necessary for true growth and expansion to occur. By persisting in giving your attention in this direction over a period of time, the anxiety will lessen, trust will develop, and then you will experience the great Truth these words can only suggest.

- *"I Am My-Self"†*

  Your Divine Being—your capital "S" Self—is Who You Truly Are. What does this True Self feel like, and where can it be found? Imagine that you are walking in a beautiful garden along an ancient stone path. The lush greenery and floral displays around you are intoxicating, and the only sounds are those of lovely bird songs and a softly burbling stream. You have been blessed to visit a primordial place of wonder in which no other soul has been for centuries. Take a few moments and fix this vision in your mind's eye. After a short while, your attention is drawn to a luminous, pure white sphere on the path up ahead. It almost looks like a star, about the size of a

---

\*   From Raj (40).

†   The "I Am My-Self Meditation" is based on teachings from the book *On Wings of Light* by Ronna Herman (26).

large animal that descended from the heavens right in front of you. Its light conveys a power and intelligence beyond description, but its glow does not blind and its heat does not burn. As you approach, its radiance begins to penetrate you, awakening a warm feeling of deep peace within. You feel the invitation to move closer, eventually moving into the sphere itself. The white light envelopes you until a point when you are no longer aware of anything outside—the garden, the birds, or the stone path. Now your entire reality is simply, but profoundly, a sense of ever-deepening peace and infinite expansion, with absolutely no physical or bodily limitations. After a while the star recedes from the garden, while you remain on the path, emanating a rarefied energy from within, surrounded by beautiful white light. You have met your Higher Self and have become one with It.

I should also mention the practice of meditation based on working with the chakras, the seven major energy centers of the body. The purpose in giving awareness to them is to bring about energy cleansing to promote physical and mental, as well as spiritual, healing. Because these practices are very powerful and require more than passing knowledge to follow them comfortably, I recommend taking the time to gather more in-depth information first.

Generally, chakra cleansing involves spending a few moments being aware of each center, visualizing its color in the sequence the centers are presented below. When you visualize the color, it is in a luminescent, shimmering form, similar to the way it looks in nature, as in a rainbow, or by a prism's refraction of light. Also, visualize a particular energy center's color where the energy center is located. After some practice, you will know a chakra's position unmistakably by the feeling of energy there. The seven major chakras, along with each one's general location and color, are as follows:

Chakra 1—Base of the Spine (Red)
Chakra 2—Pelvis (Orange)
Chakra 3—Solar Plexus (Yellow)
Chakra 4—Heart (Green)
Chakra 5—Throat (Blue)
Chakra 6—Third Eye (Indigo)
Chakra 7—Crown of the Head (Violet)

Understand that each chakra's energy is associated with the state of health in certain areas of the body. A feeling someone has of the heart breaking, for instance, is more literal than most people realize. That particular energy held in the heart chakra (number 4) on a prolonged basis could eventually become expressed physically in the form of any number of related ailments. *Anatomy of the Spirit,* by Caroline Myss (2), does a fine job of introducing the connection between emotional issues affecting the chakras and the body's physical health

The chakras also have significance for a person's spiritual evolution. Each energy center is the locus of meaning for an area of life experience. The first chakra at the base of the spine is the center concerned with physical survival; the second chakra is associated with sexual and creative drives; the third is where matters of power and mastery in the world reside. When the fourth, or heart, chakra is reached, the emphasis shifts from the material to the spiritual, with each successively higher chakra representing a more expanded state of consciousness.

Most of us spend our lives almost completely within the realm of the three lower, physically oriented chakras, but as we begin to open spiritually, we become aware of the energy inherent in the higher chakras. This ancient knowledge of human energy is intertwined with kundalini, the animating life force of the body, as I touched on earlier. Once again, if this direction of spiritual practice appeals to you, many sources of information are available that provide much more background.

## Other Ways to Find Direct Experience

There are ways of practicing besides sitting meditation that can also move you beyond concepts or beliefs, so that you may know for yourself what is Real, and uncover a sense of certainty—a North Star—from your direct experience. Just as with meditation, the aim of these practices is to clear the mind of thought so that deeper knowing may enter into your awareness. Each is followed on a routine basis for a finite amount of time, as prescribed by cultural or religious discipline or ritual. My intent here is to make you aware of alternative forms of practice that exist and encourage you to research and explore them more fully should you so desire. For a broad survey of Eastern and Western approaches to healing across the entire spectrum of human awareness, I highly recommend Ken Wilber's book, *No Boundary* (25).

- *Body Practices*

  The purposeful movement of the body has also been used in many forms since ancient times to quiet the mind and simply *be* in the present moment. While not as simple to learn as meditation, once you become proficient in a particular discipline, it can usually be practiced with the same freedom as meditation.

  Yoga, originating in the Hinduism of India, is one of the most recognized forms of meditation through motion in the West today and has numerous forms. Generally, during the practice of yoga, one assumes various postures designed to focus attention on certain areas of the body and, of course, the breathing cycle. This is done purposefully and with keen concentration so that true knowledge of the Self, and of God, can enter into the awareness. A good place to start might be *Full Catastrophe Living* (14), which describes Hatha Yoga and presents some basic practices. Hatha Yoga is a more physical form of practice and is consistent with the focus of the book, which is health improvement through stress reduction and conditioning.

Many other forms of yoga exist, including, Bhakti (emphasizing devotional religious observance), Karma (emphasizing service to mankind), and Jnana (focusing on the intellect). Kundalini Yoga was mentioned earlier as a practice to work with, and experience in a beneficial way, the cosmic energy that animates the physical body. You may choose from other disciplines; we are only scratching the surface here. Remember that yoga evolved over thousands of years into a highly effective set of practices that can eventually help one reach higher spiritual understanding and experience.

From ancient China comes Tai Chi, a system of very precise and deliberate movements that require intense concentration. Lao Tzu, in sixth century BC China, is generally thought to have begun the philosophy of Taoism, at the center of which is the Tao, the ineffable, unknowable source of All That Is. Tai Chi developed as a practice of physical, meditative movement within Taoism, mainly by watching the activities of animals and other natural phenomena. Certain martial arts based on Taoism are also considered to be expressions of Tai Chi. Like the postures in yoga, the forms in Tai Chi call for very precise positioning of the body to quiet the mind, so as to become present and promote the circulation of Chi (akin to the animating energy of kundalini) for greater vitality and health. The book *Tao of Meditation* (36) is an excellent place to learn more.

Walking meditation is similar to Tai Chi in terms of using movement, but it is much less structured. One can simply walk mindfully, in a very slow and methodical way, paying attention to the repetitive movement and the breathing cycle of the body to calm the mind. Like stationary meditation, it is simple to do and effective;

however, I offer a word of caution. If you try walking in a very slow and methodical way in your backyard, be prepared for sideways glances and odd remarks from your neighbors. (Hint: you can always say you were looking for a lost contact lens.)

- *Shamanic Practices*
Taken across many diverse native cultures, shamanism is the oldest spiritual system in the world. Its practices are as varied as the indigenous peoples who follow them. But, a common theme among them is the knowing of Spirit directly and the principle of moving beyond the mind to enable this knowing. They also consist of highly advanced "technologies of the sacred" that have been refined across the millennia. The shaman, or spiritual master, is the one within the tribe that serves as the common repository of this knowledge; he comes to receive it by daunting rites of initiation. The term "shamanic illness" has been used to describe the form of acute suffering in which one receives the call of Spirit and which must be endured until it is finally relieved by successful passage through this transformational period. At the end of this trial, the shaman is acclimatized to his or her greatly expanded perception and is ultimately accepted as the tribe's spiritual guide and healer.

Aside from the lurid and sensationalized picture commonly held about native cultures using mind-altering substances (discussed later in The Tao of Drugs in Chapter 8,) or holding voodoo rituals, many practices contain elements commonly found in other mystical traditions. Some involve physical ceremonies featuring continuous activity, such as dancing and chanting over long periods, sometimes days, to break down the barriers to mystical experience. More adept practitioners may utilize such potent tools as The Gait of Power (38) to reveal their oneness with nature and trust in Divine guidance. This activity "consists of moving at great speed [in the desert, for instance], utilizing an unusual energy, without depending on the five senses in the ordinary way and without acquiring prior knowledge of the terrain, even in complete darkness." Other techniques are highly mental, such as the Toltec procedure of Recapitulation, where the practitioner systematically records every relationship and event from his or her lifetime, and then uses this information during guided meditations to enable spiritual opening.

The essential objective of these practices is to recapture the energy necessary to trigger a fundamental shift in perception (3). In the fascinating framework of the Toltecs of Mexico, as related by Carlos Casteneda, a human being is actually an egg-shaped set of energy fields, not the physical entity we all believe ourselves to be. Countless rays of universal light emanating from the Source of Spirit, "metaphorically called the Eagle," form each egg from their radiance. "Only a very small group of the energy fields inside this luminous ball are lit up" from a spot known as the assemblage point located near the outer reaches of the egg. The position of this point is entirely responsible for which rays are experienced and, accordingly, how one perceives the energy of the Universe, including the physicality of the world and all of the events within it.[12]

The reason most of humanity shares perceptions that are so strikingly similar is because nearly all of us have had our assemblage points fixed in the same spot through ages of cultural conditioning. That is to say, we all see and experience the same rays. Spiritual opening really amounts to moving the assemblage point to a new location so that new emanations from the Eagle may be illuminated, causing new perceptions to register with us.

But, this is only possible by doing what is necessary to reclaim the vast sums of energy wasted by adhering to artificial cultural definitions of the Self, the very energy that is required for the assemblage point to be moved. The challenge is that doing what is necessary usually goes against the cultural grain and leads to a set of perceptions different from that of most other people. Although described in Toltec language and imagery, these views of conscious experience are actually very similar to the spiritual wisdom from many of the world's other esoteric bodies of knowledge.

As you might imagine, it is beyond the scope of this book to document these practices in detail. The books footnoted below will provide a good entry point into these approaches from the perspective of the native peoples of Mexico and Ecuador (2,13,38,39). Some of these authors are spiritual teachers who guide students in these practices, and periodically, lead visits to the lands of indigenous cultures for the opportunity to become temporarily immersed in their ways. Spiritual organizations in the Western world also specialize in exploring shamanic rituals and practices.

- *Religious Mysticism*
  Obscured within the great religions that originated from Abraham—Judaism, Christianity, and Islam—and their mainstream denominations, are certain practices that are much more spiritually direct in comparison to the conventional prayer services and study of law common to these faiths today. The Eastern religions are well-known for making meditation and other forms of unmediated experience part of their tradition. But, contemplative practices have played a central role in the spiritual quest within the Abrahamic religious systems, as well.

  Historically, the mystical schools of the mainstream

religions existed at the margins of conventional belief. They were generally considered to be heresy, and often were dealt with harshly by the governing religious authorities. This wisdom was not widely disseminated, either because of the real possibility that those who were not ready would misuse it or simply because it did not conform to established religious law. More recently, we have observed traditional biases eroding to an unprecedented degree as esoteric insights have gained more acceptance as valid spiritual knowledge. The rediscovery of the personal, direct experience that these teachings encourage will hopefully help to return the felt spirituality to religious traditions that many people in the west find lacking today.

For almost two thousand years, Kabbalah, the mystical branch of Judaism, enabled personal experience of the Divine and is now witnessing a resurgence of interest as people, even from outside Judaism, search for deeper spiritual meaning.*,13 Indeed, as Rabbi David Cooper points out (15), "Jewish mysticism is a profoundly sensual, nature-connected spiritual practice

---

\* Let me note that the embrace of Kabbalah by certain famous individuals, Madonna, most prominently, has provoked a controversy over the way it is being popularized today. One focus of this debate is The Kabbalah Center, an organization that teaches a version that incorporates what some have pejoratively called New Age ideas and practices. With fifty locations worldwide, it promotes the opening of Jewish Mysticism to everyone, without the years of studying Hebrew and ancient texts. Some of its claims and business practices have also been questioned. The conservative argument, espoused by several scholars of Judaism, is that the study, effort, and maturity required to truly understand and integrate this wisdom cannot be avoided. Traditionally, Kabbalah was "reserved for over-forty male scholars who have mastered Torah and Talmud." Progressive observers, on the other hand, ask why beneficial spiritual wisdom should be withheld from anyone who is ready to receive it.

that openly discusses angels and demons, the soul's journeys after death, reincarnation, resurrection, and the goal of achieving messianic consciousness." The foremost repository of Kabbalist knowledge is *The Zohar,*[14] or Book of Splendor, which was established in the thirteenth century as a record of mystical writings dating back more than one thousand years from that time.

Great Jewish mystics have shaped Kaballah through the ages, including Rabbi Isaac Luria, who taught in the sixteenth century, and whose influence on Kaballah as practiced today was considerable. It was Luria's vision that the light of the Divine was hidden within the "husks" of each and every thing during the "primordial chaos" of the creation of the world. "Every particle in our physical universe, every structure and every being, is a shell that contains sparks of holiness. Our task, according to Luria, is to release each spark from the shell and raise it up, ultimately to return it to its original state. The way these sparks are raised is through loving-kindness, of being in harmony with the universe, and through higher awareness."

In Kaballah, a foundational structure of existence underlying all creation is present, which is referred to symbolically as the Tree of Life. As Rabbi Copper explains, ten Divine emanations, called sefirot, compose the Tree, and that they individually and together define all of the characteristics of the universe and human beings. The bottom seven sefirot in the Tree are concerned with everyday awareness, while the top three represent greatly expanded levels of consciousness. Humanity can aspire to two of these three cosmic realms. Binah consciousness can be reached through the practice of meditation and the willingness to relinquish worldly attachments, with the ultimate result being a person who is living totally in the present moment and who has left the ego behind.

Cochma awareness goes further and can only be attained through Divine grace. Here, one is released from having an individual identity and lives in a continual state of infinite awareness. At the top of the Tree of Life is Keter, unreachable, unknowable, and of which nothing can be said.

Today, there is also a renewed interest in the lost gospels of Christianity—including those of Thomas, Mary, and Peter—and the beliefs of the cultures that existed close to the time of Christ, such as the Gnostics and the Thomasines.[15] Recent investigation of these non-canonical scriptures, and books such as Elaine Pagels' *Beyond Belief, The Secret Gospel of Thomas*, advance a picture of Christianity where an individual's salvation results more from direct spiritual experience than from Christ's intercession. Jesus is generally seen as one who demonstrates the inherent potential that all humans possess, that being to find the Christ Consciousness within themselves, rather than being the one through whom all humans must go to realize this possibility.

As Dr. Pagels states, "… the Gospel of Thomas teaches—that God's light shines not only in Jesus but, potentially at least, in everyone. Thomas's gospel encourages the hearer not so much to *believe in Jesus*, as John requires, as to *seek to know God* through one's own, divinely given capacity, since all are created in the image of God." These gospels, rediscovered in Egypt in 1945, actually seem to have more in common with Kabbalah than with those that would later become the foundation of the New Testament. In Pagel's view, "… Thomas expresses what would become a central theme of Jewish—and later Christian—mysticism a thousand years later: that the 'image of God' is hidden within everyone, although most people remain unaware of its presence."

Mystics of renown have visited Christianity through the growth and development of the Catholic, Eastern Orthodox, and Protestant denominations. The common theme they expressed is the transformation of consciousness that occurs when one's true, divine nature is directly experienced. Christian sages, such as Meister Eckhart from the thirteenth century and St. Theresa of Avila from the sixteenth century, have written vividly about mystical states of being. In some cases, their commentary has a striking similarity to Eastern thought, for instance, Eckhart's observation regarding the releasing of worldly attachments: "Now there are certain people who turn from things out of love, but who still have great regard for what they have left. But those who understand in truth that even when they have given themselves up and have abandoned all things, this is still absolutely nothing—those who live in this way, truly possess all things."[16]

Islam too has its mystical school, Sufism, within which there are many orders. Sufism or *tasawwuf,* as it is called in Arabic, is generally understood by scholars and Sufis to be the inner, mystical, or psycho-spiritual dimension of Islam. Rumi, who lived in thirteenth century Persia, "has been called the greatest mystical poet of any age. During a period of twenty-five years, he composed over seventy thousand verses of poetry—poetry of divine love, mystic passion, and ecstatic illumination."[17] The poems of Rumi have been rediscovered for their power in describing the experience of the Divine, and indeed, they are quoted in many of the recent books on spirituality. Here is brief, but moving example.[18]

Love rests on no foundation.
It is an endless ocean, with no beginning or end.
Imagine, a suspended ocean,

riding on a cushion of ancient secrets.
All souls have drowned in it,
and now dwell there.
One drop of that ocean is hope,
and the rest is fear.

Although the specific mystical practices within the great religions of the east and west are not expanded upon here, it's still easy to see the common threads that they share with most of the universal spiritual wisdom we have already explored. These practices are available to you, should your curiosity to learn more lead you to search in that direction.

# Chapter 8

## Cautionary Considerations

*Men are not prisoners of fate, but only prisoners of their own minds        —Franklin D. Roosevelt*

When you are walking the spiritual walk, you are likely to find that the path to awakening is not always straight and smooth. As we have seen earlier, spiritual exploration can trigger many types of unexpected growing pains you may need to work through. You may also find yourself wondering whether you should find a catalyst to accelerate the expansion of your awareness, either in the form of a spiritual teacher or the use of mind-altering drugs. Brief, but important, perspectives on three especially challenging aspects of spirituality are offered below to help you, should they become relevant in your experience.

### A Guru for You?

Throughout this book, I have been referencing the published wisdom of those who have either walked down the path of spiritual awakening, counseled others on their journeys, or who have a much larger view of Reality than most of us presently enjoy. These wise ones are certainly teaching us about spiritual awakening, but they are not usually available to us other than through their works. The flow of communication is one way, with no direct opportunity for real-time interaction. That being the case, what about the times when you need the personal attention and guidance of someone to help you through a difficult period, when bewildering changes are occurring, or when you think you are stuck and nothing is occurring at all?

Many sources offer wise advice with regard to this often misunderstood aspect of spirituality. A teacher who knows the territory you wish to traverse, and who is genuinely coming from a place of inner integrity can be a godsend. As I related earlier, for nine years, my teacher was my psychologist. She was not following a spiritual agenda and was not a spiritual teacher, strictly speaking; but she was helping me to reach a point of departure, from where I could continue the search for my Self on a new and expanded level. Moreover, my trust in her knowledge and best intentions to further my growth would be a requirement for any type of mentor relationship at any level of inquiry.

It's more problematic when it comes to spiritual advisers, however, as evidenced by the fact that we usually hear so much about the ones who are scoundrels, megalomaniacs, and narcissists. Both Eastern and Western cultures have their share of religious swindlers and cults, as has been well publicized. Nevertheless, the time may come when you need support from someone who can help you stand when spiritual confusion arises. At the point when you may be entering into uncharted waters, having a guide becomes very beneficial. The key is to avoid searching for a teacher in desperation and to be candid about what it is you are truly seeking. Do you really want spiritual clarity, or do you perhaps want a parent to protect you or a hero to worship? Instead, it might be better to trust that the right person for you will show up at the right time. As an ancient saying goes, "When the student is ready, the teacher will appear."* This is not to discourage seeking a teacher to help you (see

---

\* Thom Hartmann's personal account of his spiritual journey in *The Prophet's Way*, particularly how he met and developed a lifelong relationship with his teacher, illustrates this point very well (30).

Spiritual Emergency below, as an example), but to counsel patience and paying attention to your inner guidance to determine whether it feels like a good fit for what you truly need.

It is also worthwhile to become informed about the dynamics that are possible in a relationship with a spiritual teacher. Jack Kornfield's books, *After the Ecstasy, the Laundry* (1), and A *Path with Heart* (27), contain very insightful information on the perils, as well as the rewards, often experienced in this relationship. A particularly charismatic teacher, for example, may be mistaken for one who is also wise. Yet, great charm and wisdom do not always reside in the same individual at the same time. It's also the case that spiritual teachers with a large following may become "drunk" from all of the attention and adoration, losing their sense of mission along with their ethics. When this happens, dysfunction stemming from the teacher's behavior is likely to become evident, usually involving the misuse of any or all of power, money, sex, or drugs. After all, gurus are people, too. Some may be highly adept in their spiritual practice, but not very mature when it comes to bringing their wisdom and love into the world.

In any relationship, including one with a spiritual teacher, don't give your power away. Virtually all of the spiritual sources I have referenced stress that all true teachers are not really imparting their knowledge to you, but simply helping to awaken within you what is already your inescapable and fundamental nature. In Neale Donald Walsch's *Conversations with God* (5), God tells us something that is contrary to what we have all heard since our childhoods. Life is not really about learning lessons. It's about remembering what we already know at a very deep level within us: "Life … is an opportunity for you to know *experientially* what you already know *conceptually.* You need *learn nothing* to do this. You need merely remember what you already

> True teachers are not really imparting their knowledge to you, but simply helping to awaken within you what is already your inescapable and fundamental nature.

know, and *act on it.*" We are also reminded: "A true teacher is not
the one with the most knowledge, but the one who causes the
most others to have knowledge."

From this perspective, an enlightened master is really just
like you or me. Eckhart Tolle asks, "If only your master is an
incarnation of God, then who are you?" Then he reminds us to
"Use the master's presence to reflect your own identity beyond
name and form back to you and to become more intensely present
yourself." By keeping your divine nature in mind, and your desire
to see what is true about you more clearly, it will be easier to have
a rewarding relationship with a wise teacher while discerning one
whose problems would inhibit your spiritual growth. You will
also see that your teacher can offer great wisdom even with his or
her imperfections as an earthly human being.

In my own case, I have not pursued a personal spiritual
mentor or guru up to now, even though I have indeed had
my own burning questions and periods of disquiet. As I have
mentioned, my natural bias is one of caution, especially when
it comes to trusting someone I don't know with something as
fundamentally powerful as the realm of Spirit. It's also possible
that I am resisting further changes that would likely come from
having someone serving as my personal spiritual catalyst. Up to
this point, it has seemed best to become open to and trust in the
Divine inner teacher that I, along with everyone else, have. In the
meantime, if it becomes appropriate for a teacher to come into
my life, I'm sure I will know.

### Spiritual Emergency

*Spiritual Emergency* (35) is actually the title of an excellent book
on this subject, a compilation of essays by various authors edited
by Dr. Stanislav and Christina Grof. It may not be obvious,
but an opening to the expanded awareness of Reality can
assume many powerful forms, and the experience is not always
pleasant or smooth. The Grofs' identified several possible triggers
for spiritual emergency including, but not limited to: "the

awakening of kundalini, episodes of unitive consciousness ('peak experiences'), the crisis of psychic opening, past-life experiences, communications with spirit guides and 'channeling', and near-death experiences." A research article published in 2000 by David Lukoff[19] (and his colleagues), a noted psychologist and academic who has written extensively about spiritual issues and mental health, also summarized different classes of spiritual problems that can become spiritual emergencies:

- "Questioning of Spiritual Values"—"triggered by an experience of loss of a sense of spiritual connection."
- "Meditation-related Problems"—"altered perceptions that can be frightening, and 'false enlightenment' associated with delightful or terrifying visions" or "anxiety, dissociation, depersonalization*,[20] ... agitation and muscular tension ..."

> There are many powerful forms an opening to the expanded awareness of Reality can assume, and the experience is not always pleasant or smooth.

- "Mystical Experience"
  — "a transient, extraordinary experience marked by feelings of unity, harmonious relationship to the divine and everything in existence, as well as euphoria, sense of noesis (access to the hidden spiritual dimension), loss of ego functioning, alterations in time and space perceptions, and a sense of lacking control over the event."
- "Near-Death Experience (NDE)"—a subjective event experienced by persons who come close to death, who

---

\*    Dissociation is the sense of disconnectedness between things that normally are associated, including experiences that are usually well integrated into the self. Depersonalization is the sense of being detached or alienated from one's body, as can happen in an out-of-body experience. Derealization, a third condition sometimes associated with mystical experience, is the sense of unreality or detachment about the physical world.

are believed dead and unexpectedly recover, or who
confront a potential fatal situation and escape uninjured.
It usually includes dissociation from the physical body,
strong positive affect, and transcendental experiences."

– "Leaving a Spiritual Teacher or Path"—"transitioning
from the 'culture of embeddedness' with [spiritual]
teachers into more independent functioning ..."

These crises can occur through many different circumstances
and have the potential to greatly upset one's sense of balance.
Yet, remember that, in a larger sense, opportunities exist for
an individual's healing and continued spiritual evolution, once
the individual assimilates the meaning of a spiritual emergency
within their particular life situation. Granted, remembering this
can be a challenge in the midst of a crisis, especially one that is
longer in duration.

Joseph Campbell (33) called this "The Hero's Journey," a
willing acceptance of the call to spiritual battle. The Hero, in the
spiritual sense, is one who embarks on a voyage into the unknown
and, along the way, meets up with and faces the demons that
have long been hidden among the shadows within. Naturally, the
Hero requires much resourcefulness and perseverance to slay all
of his or her dragons, but the end of the journey sees the Hero
emerging from this trial victorious, purified, and stronger than
ever.

Another well-known illustration of the endurance of hardship
sometimes necessary to reach a higher spiritual plane is *The Dark
Night of the Soul.* [21] This was actually the title of the work by St.
John of the Cross, a Christian mystic who suffered greatly when
he tried to reform the Carmelites in sixteenth-century Spain. The
main theme of the Dark Night is that one must embrace the
desolation needed for true, Divine illumination to occur, changes
that may mean letting go of what is currently held most dear. The
idea of spiritual trial by fire is found in the mythology of cultures

the world over with the same archetypal message given through a wide variety of characters and plots.

The tales may often be myths, but they are based on the real experiences of spiritual seekers through the centuries. In Chapter 3, An Unexpected Detour, I described my own difficult episodes and the subsequent connection I made to the essential necessity of releasing fear by practicing patience, listening to intuition, and finding the higher meaning in everyday living. In my case, I held it together and came through this period, mainly because no other way was open to me. But it has crossed my mind that if things hadn't worked out, or if this confusion had not been of short duration, I would have benefited from the help of those who understand the difference between a true psychiatric problem (e.g., organic psychosis or chronic depression), and a spiritual emergency. Apparently, I'm not the only one.

The Grof's pointed out what many of us who lived through the 1960s already know. Not only was this a time of social upheaval on many fronts—reexamination of race relations, shifts in gender roles, and an eroding trust in traditions and institutions—there also developed "a wave of interest in spirituality and consciousness exploration that manifested itself in many different ways." This spiritual exploration generally ranged from, "oriental spiritual practices to experiential psychotherapies and self-experimentation with psychedelic drugs." Since the emergence of this phenomenon in the 1960s, according to the Grofs, "More and more people seem to be realizing that true spirituality is based on personal experience and is an extremely important and vital dimension of life." However, along with this, "the number of people who have experienced mystical and paranormal states has been steadily increasing … [and] it seems that the number of difficulties associated with spiritual experiences is also increasing from year to year."

A key problem for people encountering these difficulties in Western society has been the treatment given to them by the mental health profession. Psychiatry, psychology, and related fields, are by far the most well-established and socially sanctioned authorities regarding issues of perception or consciousness. Nevertheless, "traditional psychiatry makes no distinction between psychosis and mysticism and tends to treat all nonordinary states of consciousness by suppressive medication" when, in fact, "many of the states that psychiatry considers to be manifestations of mental diseases of unknown origin are actually expressions of a self-healing process in the psyche and body."

Since the Grofs published *Spiritual Emergency* in 1989, there have been indications that the traditional stance of the mental health profession is beginning to change. The Lukoff article describes these new developments, their antecedents, and various perspectives on recognizing spiritual problems. In 1994, a new diagnostic category for "Religious or Spiritual Problems" was established in an update to the *Diagnostic and Statistical Manual* of the American Psychiatric Association. Transpersonal* therapists with experience in spiritual emergencies were mainly responsible for proposing the new category, especially through "the work of the Spiritual Emergence Network [see below] to increase the competence of mental health professionals in sensitivity to such spiritual issues."

While the acknowledgment of religious and spiritual problems as a valid diagnostic category is encouraging, it is only a start. A practical concern the Lukoff paper raises is the lack of training that mental health practitioners receive to be able to discern these types of difficulties. Several studies cited indicate that this training deficiency is the rule rather than the exception. Regardless, "psychologists are very likely to work with the religious and spiritual issues of their clients [while] their lack of

---

\*    The term transpersonal refers to that which is beyond the physical and waking awareness of the individual. Carl Jung and Abraham Maslow most prominently, have included spirituality and perception beyond the body and the five senses as an integral part of the human being. Ken Wilber explains the transpersonal realm of consciousness and related therapies in his book *No Boundary* (25).

training in the assessment and treatment of religious and spiritual problems may … interfere with their ability to understand and explore their clients' issues." Also, very few published articles and case reports focus on the religious and spiritual arena. Only 364 abstracts out of over four million records in a major medical research database from the years 1980 through 1996 were related to these problems in a health care context.

Indeed, even with the current interest in direct spiritual experience, we still live in a culture almost completely circumscribed by either hyperrationality or rigid religious doctrine. With this backdrop, where should a person turn in the midst of a spiritual emergency? In our society, a caring and intuitive therapist, such as I have described in my experience, still may be the most readily available source of assistance, the concerns raised above notwithstanding. As a practical matter, it's probably easier to get a referral from a trusted friend who knows a good therapist than it would be to get one for a good spiritual teacher. But, the therapist must be open-minded enough to consider the possibility that a problem might be an unknown process that is actually a natural form of human expression, such as a spiritual opening.*

If appropriate, finding a therapist who specializes in transpersonal psychology might be the best bet to help directly with a transformational spiritual issue. As Lukoff, et al, stated, "For spiritual emergencies, most of the models of intervention come from the transpersonal psychology literature." The types

---

* Let me note that the goal of diagnosing a mental problem is not to discount the possibility of mental illness or to treat it inappropriately. In the Grofs' words, "While traditional approaches tend to pathologize mystical states, there is the opposite danger of spiritualizing psychotic states and glorifying pathology or, even worse, overlooking an organic problem. Transpersonal counseling is not appropriate for conditions of a clearly psychotic nature, characterized by lack of insight, paranoid delusions and hallucinations, and extravagant forms of behavior."

of recommended therapeutic approaches include having "the person temporarily discontinue more active inner exploration and all forms of spiritual practice, change their diet to include more 'grounding foods' (such as red meat), become involved in very simple grounding activities (such as gardening), [and] engage in regular light exercise (such as walking)." On the whole, "Reliance on the client's self-healing capacities is one of the main principles that guides the transpersonal treatment of spiritual emergencies."

The differences between an acute episode, such as mine, and more chronic problems are also important to consider. Many people have experienced extended periods of debilitating depression and psychological misery because they have immersed themselves for long stretches of time in spiritual practice. Jack Kornfield emphasizes the need to recognize that these "dark nights," if they come, are as much a part of our spiritual journey as the illumination and bliss. In his book, *After the Ecstasy, the Laundry* (1), are many tales of spiritual practitioners who sank to depths every bit as awful in degree as the rapturous heights they previously had scaled. However, nearly all of these accounts resulted in a deeper, more rounded wisdom, one not possible by having the bliss alone.

What this means in terms of the treatment of an extended Dark Night is found in a common story line that runs through most of these cases. These people had usually been following an intense form of disciplined practice as a central part of their daily routine, sometimes continuing for years in monasteries or on extended retreats. They eventually reached a state in their cloistered environment where they were able to maintain greatly expanded levels of conscious awareness on a prolonged basis. But, even with all of the enlightenment, for various reasons, they arrived at the realization that their lives were incomplete without the experience of the world of culture—employment, romance, possessions, money, etc.—and all of the attachments and challenges it can bring.

Decisions were made to reenter the world after years of seclusion, and that's when the problems began. When conflicts arose in relationships or from juggling the bills, for instance, it became very difficult for them to cope after the singular focus on their spiritual practice. Often, they experienced profound guilt or fear because of the self-imposed expectation that they should automatically demonstrate advanced spiritual insight in any environment or set of circumstances. Knee-jerk responses of anger, frustration, attachment, and so on, were hard to accept in these people who had, in some cases, devoted decades to their daily discipline. What they ultimately learned is that similarly long periods were sometimes required of them to assimilate the ways of the world back into their psyches. The lesson in all of these experiences, as Kornfield reminds us, is that spiritual growth does not happen only in isolation and must be practiced every day in every situation for true spiritual maturity to develop.

Therapy in this context of prolonged anxiety or depression, in my view, would be well served by more traditional approaches, even if the problem had its roots in a spiritual crisis. In these situations, we are not dealing with the short-term harnessing of unfamiliar bursts of energy or getting through episodes of panic triggered by powerful mystical encounters. Here, we are talking about just coping day to day until, with compassion and patience, all of the disconnected threads of experience from two seemingly very different realms can be integrated. This is consistent with the basic goal of most forms of Western psychotherapy, which is, simply stated, to help a person become more functional in the world. Once the person's feet are back on the ground, spiritual practice potentially may be resumed in a way that would offer a much broader perspective also encompassing all of the dynamics inherent in daily existence. Most importantly, the person will have learned to be accepting of the fact that he or she, like most human beings, has an ego, and the belief that this is somehow a mark of shame can be released.

A second source of spiritual guidance might be the clergy

in any of the mainstream religions. Many would say that this is part of their job description, although the same cautionary notes sounded previously about strict adherence to religious doctrine apply. If the priest, rabbi, or minister, for instance, does not treat you as an individual with specific needs, and attempts to force-fit your situation into a set of theological precepts, you will be no better off. Worse, you may end up feeling guilty and even more confused. However, like therapists, many sensitive and caring clergy will treat a bewildering spiritual problem with compassion, putting beliefs aside as much as possible. Some have training as therapists and family counselors, in addition to their spiritual background, and may actually be ideal for your needs. The key, as with spiritual teachers, is to be as discerning and honest as you can about what you want out of the relationship.

Beyond the traditional sources of counseling in times of spiritual emergency—therapists, clergy, and family doctors, who are becoming an anachronism—how else can one locate a guide who knows this territory? It was suggested before that the process of spiritual awakening itself would determine how and when an appropriate teacher would appear. Of course, the next step in the process could be revealed to you as one where you must take the initiative. Up until recently, if you were having a crisis and wanted to begin a search for someone to help, you might have considered contacting the Spiritual Emergence Network. Christina Grof founded this organization in 1980 to develop a network of mental health resources able to offer support to individuals experiencing difficulties with spiritual growth. The mission, history, and evolution of SEN are discussed in the Grofs' book.

Unfortunately, upon investigating further* I found that SEN was disbanded, presumably due to lack of funding. I have had no personal experience with this service, but the stated vision and

---

\* As of December 2003. SEN was most recently affiliated with the California Institute of Integral Studies.

approach for helping someone find a knowledgeable guide when it's not otherwise obvious how to do so, is a very compassionate and timely one. It's my hope that a similar service becomes available once again. In the meantime, without this type of aid, one could try some careful research to see if any other suitable organizations assume this clearinghouse role.

Another worthwhile activity is to become educated in what a spiritual emergency is and avail yourself of the insights others have to offer. I have referred to three valuable sources of information here, and other good ones are available, as well. But, be careful not to dwell on this information too much. After all, the primary objective is to leave the fear behind so that you may welcome your spiritual evolution. I didn't really look seriously at this information until I needed it, and at times, I thought it best for my own good to stop reading it. Once more, listen to your gut to know when to pick it up and when to put it down.

With all of this being said, a nagging question begs to be asked. Why would anyone want to risk seeking enlightenment if earnest spiritual practice could possibly lead someone into a mental and emotional train wreck? Kornfield's lesson about embracing dramatic suffering, should it appear, to become a more spiritually mature individual, wouldn't seem to be worth the price to most people. At an even more basic level is the view of many spiritual disciplines, such as the orders of Buddhism and other religions Kornfield draws wisdom from, that states of enlightenment are transitory, and to cling to them inevitably brings the same imbalances as clinging to worldly attachments do. Enlightenment is essentially a mystery people must accept on its own terms. Permanent illumination is the ultimate aim, but there don't seem to be very many, if any, individuals who have actually reached this exalted state of being

However, a subtle but very important variation on the theme of spiritual evolution is espoused by many of the sources I referenced earlier, Raj (40) and Eckhart Tolle (29) among them. They all do agree with the spiritual systems above that enlightenment can only come through surrender of personal will and being completely in the present moment. And all agree that reaching this level of awareness will usually take a long time for most people, simply because of the state of "endarkenment" we have collectively been accustomed to for so long.

But, these teachers do see an end state of sorts, one where a person will eventually awaken completely to his or her true identity, which is infinite and eternal. Going back to visit the world of limitation will then be a conscious choice, not a seemingly capricious event. According to this view of spiritual evolution, no requirement or predetermination exists that you must endure suffering to know who you truly are. You can release the karma and sins of the past, no matter how long they have been accumulating, any time you make the decision to do so. Finally, Divine purpose enters the picture in that a transformational shift in the mass consciousness of humanity is close at hand. Awakening will not be as rare or as elongated a process as in the past, and will flourish, as it becomes the rule rather than the exception.

Even with the promise of making a permanent transition and not having to suffer any more, it still can seem to be a daunting proposition to risk the trials and tribulations to get there. But, once you have had a glimpse of who you really are, your calculation of cost and benefit will change. You will know, even when the illumination fades, the Truth you saw in the Light. Inescapably, you will know that the Truth is still there, that there really is nothing else, and that you will persist, with patience, to experience yourself from that vantage point. Also, while you aren't sure when your "Hero's Journey" will commence or where it will lead, you will have one at some juncture. In the end, you will rely on your inner resources, and you will find that that they will be there for you.

> You will know, even when the illumination fades, the Truth you saw in the Light. Inescapably, you will know that the Truth is still there, and that there really is nothing else.

## The Tao of Drugs

When we talk about the use of drugs, other than for accepted medical purposes, the conversation usually centers on its cultural dimensions. Drugs have become highly integrated into various social rituals across a broad spectrum of society. From jazz musicians smoking marijuana in the 1950s to teenagers using ecstasy at nightclubs in the 2000s, drugs are a ubiquitous, if not welcome, part of the scenery. We usually frame our discussions about this phenomenon in moral or legal terms, with particular interest in how the abuse and misuse of

> We may not see what happens to our personal energy when we indulge in drugs, and the effect may be short lived, but we do become even more removed from the Truth about ourselves.

drugs can hamper one's ability to function in society, or detract from one's character. The subject of addiction also comes into play, again with a focus on the lack of control when in the grip of a chemical or psychological dependency. There are numerous demographic, psychological, and medical studies, as well as popular observations, on the subject of drugs, most of which have at least some degree of cultural perspective.

But, historically, another important dimension to the use of foreign substances has been evident: the desire of individuals to induce altered states of mind that would allow on-demand transcendence of the limited awareness believed to be an inherent feature of the material world. During the America of the 1960s, the promise of being able to do this in a controlled fashion was one of the reasons psychedelic drugs, such as LSD and derivatives of natural hallucinogens (e.g., Mescaline and Psilocybin) initially became popular.

After LSD was first synthesized in the 1940s and its mind-altering properties recognized, scientific inquiry began in earnest during the 1950s.* Soon, researchers at major universities were doing experiments using these agents as part of an overall effort to unlock the mysteries of the human mind. By the late 1960s, as social upheaval pervaded the country in the form of the anti-Vietnam War movement, urban rioting, and the assassination of several of the country's leaders, this research became a symbol for the chaos of the times and these substances were quickly and emphatically banned.

Still, word of this research had captured the imagination of several early adopters and opinion leaders, mainly in university, entertainment, and literary settings. It wasn't long before a certain mystique developed around these drugs with illegal production and distribution channels stepping in to satisfy the increasing curiosity and demand. But, instead of being employed in the spirit of the original research, they developed into a symbol of identification for the counterculture movement, a shared expression of a new lifestyle in opposition to traditional institutions. After the war, and in the decades since, drug use became less a statement of dissatisfaction with established societal norms, than a way to assuage social anxiety, escape from the weight of personal suffering or to act out the rebelliousness of adolescence.

Another historical thread, however, pertains to the use of mind-altering substances to realize expanded consciousness that has little to do with the American experience. For many of the world's native peoples, using naturally occurring substances to aid in their direct encounter of nonphysical reality is a deeply ingrained element of sacred ritual that has existed, in many cases, for centuries. John Perkins (39) writes about mystical journeys that

---

\*    John Horgan's book *Rational Mysticism* (32) describes the history of psychedelic drug research, how these agents affect the brain, their use in pursuit of expanded consciousness, and the colorful characters who brought these substances into our awareness.

he and his Western companions took after imbibing Ayahuasca*
while participating in the spiritual ceremonies of the Shuar in
the Amazon rain forest. As explained by a Shuar tribesman,
Ayahuasca, or "the Vine of the Soul," is a most important gateway
to the realm of the spirits: "They are here with us all the time. We
know them in our dreaming. We can feel them, as Jesus Christ
did, but sometimes it is difficult to see them when we are not
dreaming. Ayahuasca helps us."

Among their experiences was a profound sense of unity with
the earth and cosmos. Perkins recounts: "I felt completely at
one with the forest, the mud, and the night around me. I could
see deep into the earth herself, could feel energy pulsating up
from the layers and layers of shimmering minerals, could hear
the magma bubbling, smell the molten lava, taste the greenness
of life, and could at the same time hear the song of the distant
stars, as though the universe outside and inside the earth were
connected in some way that I had never before imagined but
that now seemed obvious and practical and so very much a part
of me." He goes on to describe his communication with the wind
and trees, and being with nature holistically on a vastly expanded
plane.

According to Joseph Campbell,[22] the rituals of the Indians in

---

\*    This potion can be brewed from several different plants, although
there are "two species most commonly associated with Ayahuasca"
(32). "Renowned Harvard botanist Richard Shultes ... collected
samples of ayahuasca's constituent plants and analyzed them in
the 1940s. Shultes, who first described ayahuasca in print in 1951
and consumed the drug himself more than twenty times, high-
lighted the great mystery posed by ayahuasca: How did the Indians
figure out that two plants that are marginally psychoactive when
consumed individually become intensely psychoactive when consumed together? By all accounts a hard-nosed rationalist, Shultes
said he could not discount the Indians' claim that their ancestors
learned how to brew the sacred potion from the spirits of the ayahuasca plants."

Northwestern Mexico have a similar mission to the Shuar's, to embark on "an inward journey, when you leave the outer world behind and come into the realm of spiritual beings." They follow elaborate procedures to "hunt" Peyote, which they associate with a sacred animal. To these Indians, the Peyote brings forth "not simply a biological, mechanical, chemical effect but one of spiritual transformation." Many other examples from all over the world exist.

Although the ability of these substances to help bring about expanded states of consciousness is well documented, it is also very important to understand the context in which they are used in indigenous societies. They are to not be taken lightly and certainly not to be used for entertainment or recreation. The people in native cultures that employ these substances, and not all do,* are aware of them from childhood and would not be likely to use them frivolously.

In fact, it may be that two individuals, one from the Amazon rain forest and one from Manhattan, taking the same drug in the same dose, would have very different reactions because of their highly ingrained cultural beliefs and perceptions. The Amazonian's experience would likely be predictable, even if otherworldly, in the sense that multidimensional consciousness is accepted as being normal and an integral part of spiritual practice. This person has been acculturated to the use of what Stanislav Grof calls (6) the "technology of the sacred" and is well prepared for its effects. The Westerner, having no comparable grounding, may have any number of outcomes, some pleasurable, some frightening, and perhaps even some that are, indeed, recognized as spiritual.

We should remember, as Joseph Campbell cautions, that "It is a terrifying experience to have your consciousness transformed."

---

\* A case in point is the Wirrarika of Central Mexico who believe "that any kind of ritual would produce empty results if it had no direct relation with the warrior's battle that we wage in the everyday world, in which the enemy to vanquish is ourselves and our limitations."(38)

It is his observation that "a mechanically induced mystical experience" is different from the real article, and essentially demands "dealing with [the] problem of the difference between the mystical experience and the psychological crack up. The difference is that the one who cracks up is drowning in the water in which the mystic swims. [One has] to be prepared for this experience."

Seth (24) goes further, warning that bypassing the ego synthetically by way of mind-altering drugs, especially with large doses of LSD, is a mistake and strongly admonishes against it. "Here we are dealing with an artificial and forced method of, hopefully, bringing about physical, psychic, and spiritual illumination." This is motivated by an erroneous belief "that the self must shed its ego and die symbolically in order that the inner self can be free." However, "When large doses of chemicals are used, the conscious mind is confronted full blast with very potent experiences that it was not meant to handle, and by which it is purposely made to feel powerless." As a result, "Consciousness finds itself in a crisis situation; not from the exterior world, but because it is forced to fight on a battleground for which it was never designed and cannot understand, where basically counted-upon allies of association, memory, and organization, and all the powers of the inner self, are suddenly turned into enemies."

My few experiences with psychedelic drugs* as a teenager that I touched on early in the book bear out Seth's and Campbell's points for me. Except for the last time, the four or five trips I took were highly exhilarating adventures in enhanced perception. I experienced wonderfully exotic views of mundane scenes, such as seeing everything in the room where I was sitting brightly outlined in neon colors. A floor made of small, intricately designed tiles

---

\* I recall believing, in all cases, that the drug was Mescaline, the chemical synthesized from the Peyote buttons of a small cactus that grows in Mexico and the Southwest United States. However, given the lack of standards and control over the production of illegal drugs, it could easily have been LSD.

suddenly became a rotating whirlpool, with the tiles disappearing down into its vortex. The feelings others reported of having an intuitive understanding of the meaning of the universe, and incredible bliss and peace, became real to me. Listening to music revealed synesthetic dimensions of sensory stimulation I never knew existed, like seeing the musical notes I was hearing paraded in front of me in vivid color. In short, many characteristics of expanded perception similar to those developed in the course of disciplined spiritual practice seem to have been accessible to me by inducing them artificially. Of course, they departed once my brain had processed the chemicals, and because I had no knowledge of the natural ways to invite and sustain higher consciousness, the only way to make them return would have been to take more chemicals.

The last trip, however, was not so pleasant. This time when I sat down to enjoy some music the songs influenced me differently than they had before. They were vaguely uncomfortable to listen to at first. Then they quickly progressed to being quite disturbing. Finally, they became unbelievably terrifying and culminated with my mind's eye seeing in very graphic and paralyzing detail what I took to be the devil. Perhaps I had opened a perceptual doorway to the realm of malevolent archetypes that Carl Jung, Stanislav Grof (6), and others describe. Whatever it was caused me to rip off my headphones and spend the rest of the night with my arms around my knees in panic, rocking back and forth promising God, "I'll never do it again," over and over and over. I spent the entire next day leaning on my best friend while he tried to help me escape from the powerful grip of this harrowing experience. Since then, I have never again touched any such substances.

To provide contrast to the Western approach, Seth describes the orientation of certain American Indians regarding the use of psychoactive substances. "Within their native framework, some American Indians use Peyote in their own way—but not as gluttons, stunning and annihilating their systems. They accept it as a natural ingredient belonging to their earthly structure. They do not try to blast themselves out of existence. They use it to increase the innate perceptions that they have. They become part of All That Is—as they should—without dying as they are. They are able to assimilate their knowledge, to purposefully direct it into both their individual lives and their social structure. They also use it within their own system of beliefs, of course, in which their creaturehood is understood and taken for granted. The conscious mind is seen as a complement, rather than a detriment, to biological being."

In the modern world, we have become considerably removed from nature, not only physically, but also spiritually. Our highly developed egos have made it difficult to pierce this veil of artificiality, so many people have sometimes turned to psychedelic substances to make it easier. But, there really are no shortcuts. Without naturally removing attention from the ego and the false identity it has assumed, using drugs for spiritual growth could actually be quite dangerous. In fact, any type of ego-oriented venture into the Divine can be unpleasant, as I already described concerning the practice of intense meditation in the absence of a spiritual purpose.

It is fascinating how drug induced mystical encounters, both blissful and terrifying, can appear at first to be so similar to those experienced from natural forms of spiritual exploration. Sometimes, I am struck by how alike the raw feelings are when I compare the memories of my teenage trips and my more recent spiritual openings during meditation. Ironically, it may be that certain hallucinogens actually stimulate the areas of brain that can be considered spiritual gateways, and because of this, it could be an especially risky proposition to use them. Bypassing the natural process of spiritual growth, which is specific to each individual, can leave powerful, mystical encounters disconnected from the rest of the psyche, and this can only position one further away from the enlightenment he or she is pursuing. Therefore, unless you are very clear about where you are on your spiritual path, or unless truly expert guidance is available, I strongly recommend avoiding the use of foreign substances to have spiritual experiences.

As for drug use in general, we may not see what happens to our personal energy when we indulge and the effect may be short lived, but we do become even more removed from the Truth about ourselves. Of course, a quick escape can feel pretty good sometimes. But once again, it comes down to making a choice: whether you want to feel pretty good, or know yourself someday as you truly are, fully aware of your freedom from limitation.

# Chapter 9

## Conceptual Guide
## —A Survey of Spiritual and Scientific Resources

> There is something I do not know, the knowing
> of which could change everything.
> —*Werner Erhard*

Great wisdom has been offered to us through the ages by a variety of teachers. Each has given, basically, the same essential messages, saying there is much more to Reality than meets the eye and all is not as it seems. Love is the basic energy of the Universe, and the present moment is all there really is. We Humans are actually infinite, multidimensional, and eternal. We have the power and responsibility to experience what God is presently Being in any way we choose. The world we see is a direct result of our choices, even if we do not make them consciously. Perhaps most important, each one of us is ultimately our own teacher and, within the laws of the Universe, physical and nonphysical, we have absolute free will in every aspect of our existence.

Particular teachings offer different perspectives to explain the same universal knowledge, with each being valuable to help us in the many aspects of spiritual growth. One such view focuses on how the universe works and what principles actually govern our existence. When you find yourself resonating with this information at a deep level, it opens doors of understanding that are quite liberating. It's also amazing to consider that the esoteric knowledge of the ages, within reach of only the select few for thousands of years, has appeared in our bookstores and on the Internet in just the past two or three decades and is now available to millions in easy-to-understand language.

It's amazing that the esoteric knowledge of the ages, within reach of only the select few for thousands of years, has just lately mushroomed throughout our bookstores and across the Internet.

Another view is a personal one, where authors describe their life experiences, how their spiritual paths unfolded, and what lessons they learned as a result. These sources can be very powerful, since the intimate nature of the author's journey usually comes through in the writing. It's also very helpful to one who is having some bewilderment and confusion around spiritual issues receive enlightening insights from others who have already been down this road.

Other variations include medical or scientific perspectives that go beyond the conventional positions of these disciplines. Usually, the author is a doctor who has had personal spiritual experiences and had the courage and curiosity to pursue knowledge outside the boundaries of what his or her peers considered acceptable. Sometimes, a scientist realizes that his or her work points to great mysteries, especially in the realm of physics. Many of these authors are highly respected in their fields and have a genuine desire to explore the boundaries between science and consciousness. Their work helps us to see that science doesn't really end with the purely materialistic, and that someday, most of us will arrive at a more holistic view of reality.

Wisdom is also available from many groups of indigenous people around the world who live a highly spiritual existence every day. Although they may follow different customs and practices, generally speaking, they share a common love and respect for the earth and for all of nature. They view the status of the animal, plant, and mineral kingdoms as equal to man's, and actually understand that the planet itself is a living being, not a collection of inanimate materials. Their worldview and spiritual experiences are sometimes very consistent with other spiritual sources, including the core wisdom of the world's great religions.

As far as the great religions are concerned, they fundamentally share the common themes of universal love. Although these teachings have become largely obscured over the centuries by manmade dogma, they are present nonetheless. The great masters who founded and guided the religions were teachers who communicated the divine laws and principles revealed to them. They taught that enlightenment comes from within, where one is one's own teacher. Great wisdom resides at the center of all the religions, even though it is the differences among religions that are typically emphasized.

Finally, I want to point out a few things regarding channeled works. Lee Carroll (11) defines channeling as, "The divine, inspired words (or energy) of God as imparted to Humans by Humans." Ultimately, the humans doing the channeling are communicating with some inter-dimensional aspect of themselves. If you find that you have some discomfort with this idea, I would ask that you give your attention to the information and, for the time being, forget about its source. Instead, decide for yourself whether these works promote individual power and responsibility, unconditional love, and elegant answers to complex questions. I think that, for the most part, they do. You may also want to consider that the essential wisdom of the great religions was channeled. After all, where else could the divine information have come from that humans recorded in the great books? If you accept this idea, it then becomes a question of whether you think Spirit and humans stopped communicating centuries ago. If these works inspire you by speaking to the God in you, it makes no difference where they originate.

Here, then, are some selected sources of spiritual and scientific information that I have found particularly enlightening. I believe many of these to be wonderful places to set sail on a spiritual journey. However, above all else, remember that you are your own highest teacher, and no one else can know what truly resonates with you. Jump in and enjoy!*

1. *After the Ecstasy, the Laundry* by Jack Kornfield
   The author is a Western psychologist who had lived as a Buddhist monk in Southeast Asia for many years. As in *A Path With Heart* (see below), Kornfield's deep spiritual wisdom comes through very clearly. In this book, he explores the nature of spiritual awakening and what it means to live in the world as it happens. The stories of many people are told, especially of long-time teachers and practitioners who relate how they came to wake up and the rewards and challenges they faced as they continued to grow. Kornfield shows common elements occur within most of these experiences, and they can provide signposts for others who have yet to follow. And, of course, once we have awakened, he reminds us that the laundry (the world we live in) will still be waiting for us. This is, perhaps, his most important point: to remember that true spiritual maturity comes not only from the inner discovery of great truths, but also through our relationships with others in the flow of everyday living.

2. *Anatomy of the Spirit* by Caroline Myss, PhD

---

\* I have chosen not to use one of the standard bibliography formats. Instead, I have ordered the references by title believing this approach to be friendlier for someone searching for content that specifically meets their present needs.

Dr. Myss is a medical intuitive who uses spiritual wisdom from world religions—Eastern and Western—as metaphors to explore the connection between mind, body, and spirit. As a medical intuitive, she can read a person's energy and determine the nonphysical causes of a medical or emotional problem before it manifests physically. The first part of the book is about her awakening and provides insight into what it's like to discover and live with a well-developed spiritual ability. Along the way, she also shares compelling stories of people who encounter life-altering spiritual events that are very helpful in understanding the nature of the spiritual quest. This is one of the first books I read about spirituality, and one that inspired me to want to know more.

3. *Art of Dreaming, The* by Carlos Casteneda
   This is one of several books by Carlos Casteneda on his relationship with Don Juan, the Yaqui Indian master. He describes many of his fantastic adventures in nonphysical reality, as well as spiritual knowledge that is consistent with indigenous wisdom from other areas of the world. The accounts of his travels throughout Mexico and the Southwest United States are also engrossing. Sprinkled throughout his books are the actual practices central to the Nagual's (spiritual master) goal of reclaiming the energy that has been tied up in maintaining worldly dreams, a necessity for reaching enlightenment. Victor Sanchez (see *Toltecs of the New Millennium* below) has distilled these practices into a single book *The Teachings of Don Carlos.**

---

\* I should mention that some people question whether Don Juan really existed or was actually an elaborate hoax perpetrated by Casteneda. From what I have read, there is no clear evidence of this, but much about Casteneda seems to be shrouded in mystery. All I can offer is that his books rang true to me, and I thought much of

4. *Brief History of the Universe, A* by Stephen Hawking

   This is perhaps the best-known book explaining the frontiers of physical science in layman's terms, written by the eminent cosmologist and expert on black holes. Hawking delves into the mysteries of the very large (stars, black holes, relativity) and the very small (subatomic theory and experimentation). He describes the mind-bending concepts that scientists confront, firing up our imagination, and showing us that even on the objective level of science, the mysterious and paradoxical are often the rule rather than the exception.

5. *Conversations with God—Book 1* by Neale Donald Walsch

   This book is a great place to begin to understand many of life's mysteries. This is the first in a series of channeled works by Neale Donald Walsch where God (or an enlightened nonphysical entity) shares wisdom on the meaning of it all and how everything really works. Regardless of whether you believe channeling is real, the content is full of sanity and amazing insights on a variety of personal and universal subjects. Some truly transformational moments will be yours if you are ready to shine new light on old beliefs. This is one of the few books I have recommended to people when they are confronting major, life-changing events and are struggling to find the meaning in them.

6. *Cosmic Game, The* by Stanislav Grof

   Stanislav Grof, a classically trained psychiatrist, began his study of human consciousness in the 1950s and has been one of the leading lights in the field ever since. This book synthesizes information from an amazing

---

the information, while using different terminology, was very similar conceptually to other spiritual perspectives. Also, others claim to have incorporated his ideas into successful spiritual practices (i.e., V. Sanchez).

variety of disciplines—religion, mythology, science, medicine, psychology, history, professional research, and personal experience—to develop a lucid description of the spiritual landscape and the place of spirituality in relationship to institutionalized systems of thought. Dr. Grof writes with uncommon wisdom and sensitivity, especially when it comes to the challenges people who are awakening spiritually have in modern society. It's quite evident that he knows about these challenges on a personal level, and his work provides a critically needed counterbalance to the orthodoxy of science and religion. This is a well-written, insightful, and courageous treatise on the human spirit.

7. *Course in Miracles, A* Foundation for Inner Peace
This is a channeling of Jesus over a seven-year period beginning in 1965 by Helen Schucman, who was a professor of medical psychology at Columbia University in New York City and a self-described atheist. She and her boss at Columbia, William Thetford, endured a highly antagonistic working relationship and jointly decided that they had to find a new way to relate to each other. Soon after, Helen began to receive the course, which William transcribed into written form. Its basic purpose is to reestablish the core truths that Jesus taught which have been lost through centuries of misunderstanding. Much of the language has a Christian orientation, but the themes discussed are universal and do not have their source in Christian religious doctrine. There are three sections, beginning with the course itself, which is written in such a way as to allow transformation of the reader at a level beyond the words. The other sections cover the personal application of, and teaching of, the course. It takes commitment to assimilate this profound wisdom, but it is well worth the investment.

8. *Creating Health* by Deepak Chopra, MD
   During the 1990s, Chopra made a name for himself as the author of many books promoting a holistic view of the human being, one where physical health originates in mind and spirit. Coming from a traditional medical background, he courageously challenged the conventional wisdom of his profession. In this book, he makes the compelling case that a healthy mind and spirit are essential for healthy body, more so than any other factor. He also shares personal casework and anecdotes across a wide spectrum of disease that bears out this idea.

9. *Dark Side of the Light Chasers, The* by Debbie Ford
   A wonderful book that shows us how all of the things we hate about ourselves are really gifts waiting to be accepted and discovered. If this sounds like pie-in-the-sky soft-headedness, you will be surprised at how practical and transformational this information really is. Essentially, Ford makes a convincing case that every human is really the totality of all possible states of being—positive, negative, and everything in between—and that pushing away the parts of ourselves we would rather not look at is the source of all of our pain. Owning all sides of ourselves is not an exercise in admitting our inadequacy or lack of goodness; it's nothing less than the pathway to wisdom and enlightenment. What makes this a possibility rather than a pipedream to the reader are the personal experiences Ford relates, as well as the meditations and exercises that are available throughout the book. This is truly a valuable work that brings a fresh, tangible approach to finding personal freedom.

10. *Diet for a New America* by John Robbins
    This is the book that convinced me to become a vegetarian. The first part of the book acquaints us with the nature of

each animal (cow, pig, chicken) that provides each type of meat (beef, pork, foul), showing them as intelligent, sentient beings deserving of kindness, even if they are raised ultimately to be slaughtered for food. It then proceeds to describe what the food processing industry has become and what it does to millions of these animals every day (*not* your father's farm). The second part of the book delves into the health benefits of eliminating animal fat from the diet and debunks many of the myths that have been propagated by self-serving industry and political interests for decades. The fact that the author was an heir to the Baskin and Robbins ice cream fortune makes his assertions all the more credible. If you decide to read this book, be prepared to spend time thinking about the welfare of these animals, as well as the effect of animal fat in your body.

11. *End Times (Kryon, Book 1), The* by Lee Carroll
This book is the first in a series by Lee Carroll, who since the late 1980s has channeled Kryon, a nonphysical entity who has been helping to prepare the earth for humanity to awaken at this critical point in our evolution. This information about our impending individual and global enlightenment, and our true multidimensional nature, while highly consistent with the other channeled works, explains more of what is occurring in today's world situation and why. Kryon also provides fascinating explanations and guidance on phenomena currently beyond our scientific understanding. His underlying message is that the path humanity has been following for thousands of years, and all of the ancient prophecies that served as signposts along the way, have recently been voided. We have embarked on new path, and must now create new signposts where none currently exists. Other

Kryon channelings and materials are also available at www.kryon.com.

12. *Father Joe* by Tony Hendra
This is a moving, funny, and brilliantly written memoir by one of the former managing editors of *National Lampoon* magazine and the creator of many other memorable satirical works. In the background throughout Mr. Hendra's eventful life is the ubiquitous Father Joseph Warrilow, a Dominican monk who counsels him through turbulent events, beginning with his exposure, at the age of fourteen, of being in a sexual liaison with another man's wife. Father Joe was the antithesis of the other religious authorities typically present during the author's upbringing in England during the 1950s, figures who often relied on cruel methods to keep young sinners in line. Unlike them, peace and calm radiated from this man. Judgment and guilt never accompanied his guidance, only the encouragement to love one's self and to see the Divine in all things. Besides this uplifting spiritual message being consistent with that in my book, Baby Boomers who came of age in the 1960s and 1970s will find Hendra's tales of reaching adulthood and helping to define the popular culture of the times particularly fascinating.

13. *Four Agreements, The* by Don Miguel Ruiz
This is the shortest of this Toltec master's books, but one with a very powerful message on how to live life for maximum inner peace and happiness. You only need to remember four things each day: be impeccable with your word, don't take anything personally, never assume anything, and try your best. There is much more meaning to these deceptively simple statements than meets the eye. Understanding and using them will liberate you from all

you thought you knew about yourself and the world we are all dreaming.

14. *Full Catastrophe Living* by Jon Kabat-Zinn, PhD
    This book is written by a well-respected researcher who has instituted pioneering stress management programs based on meditation and yoga at the University of Massachusetts Medical School. Even with a more mainstream medical orientation, he shows that direct experience of the Self is a key component in any effective healing process. Kabat-Zinn offers many words of wisdom and practical guidance on working meditation, yoga, and relaxation techniques into your daily life.

15. *God Is a Verb* by Rabbi David A. Cooper
    Rabbi Cooper shares the teachings of Kabbalah, the mystical branch of Judaism. Many Jewish stories and parables are also very consistent with the core wisdom from other religions and sources of spiritual knowledge. Being raised as a Jew myself, these stories really resonated with me. This was one of the books that helped me understand the importance of making the commitment to bring spiritual awareness into everyday situations and relationships.

16. *Hidden Lives of Dogs, The* by Elizabeth Thomas Marshall
    Marshall provides wonderful insights into the nature of dogs with which we have shared our existence for the last fifteen thousand years. This book also contains accounts of canine behavior showing that Humans don't by any means have a monopoly on intelligence. Two of the author's other books I have read, *The Social Lives of Dogs* and *The Tribe of the Tiger* (about cats large and small), are every bit as good as this one. These books open us up to

how important it is to consciously bring an appreciation of animals (and all of nature) back into our lives.

17. *Holographic Universe, The* by Michael Talbot
Some leading scientists say that our knowledge of the subatomic world suggests the universe is really holographic in nature. Every component of the universe (planets, people, atoms) has information about the whole embedded in it. This is in alignment with the spiritual truth that all is one, and that what underlies the physical world is a nonphysical one from which everything originates. This work is largely based on the work of David Bohm, the renowned physicist and Einstein protégé, and Karl Pribram, the pioneering neurophysiologist, who has mapped many of the brain's functions since the 1960s. Each independently came to the same basic conclusions, even though their approaches were based on very different scientific disciplines.

18. *Hyperspace* by Michio Kaku
This is one of my favorites of the cosmology-for-laymen genre. The author writes with uncommon clarity and explains the recent thinking that has emerged at the forefront of physics, including superstring theory and multidimensional model of the Universe. Here we learn that, according to the most advanced mathematical models, at least ten dimensions exist in the universe. Not only does he address current theories, but Kaku also covers the history of scientific discovery, enlightening us about why the last few decades have been so revolutionary and controversial regarding our perception of the universe. For a spiritual seeker, it is gratifying to observe scientific inquiry continuing to suggest that there is always much more to the universe than could ever be contained in our best rational understanding.

19. *Kundalini, Evolution and Enlightenment* Edited by John White
    This is a comprehensive compilation of writings on the subject of kundalini—what it is, personal accounts, research, advice, and more. The authors are from a wide spectrum of disciplines from the spiritual to the literary. This is a valuable resource for someone who wants to know more about the energy of the Divine that animates our physical existence, as well as the consequences of awakening this energy too rapidly.

20. *Last Hours of Ancient Sunlight, The* by Thom Hartmann
    Most of this book makes an eye-opening case that modern civilization is about to exhaust the oil that it took nature millions of years to create, and how and why our condition came to be. It is well researched and particularly fascinating when it comes to the relationship between population and energy use, and the increasing threat to modern existence as recent population thresholds have been surpassed. The last part of the book ties the coming crisis to the need for human awakening to change the dead-end we have been approaching. It is a fresh perspective on an old problem that is disturbing, but illuminating.

21. *Life of Pi* by Yann Martel
    This recent novel (published in 2001) is ostensibly about a young Indian man who finds himself adrift on a twenty-six-foot lifeboat in the Pacific Ocean with a four-hundred-and-fifty-pound Bengal tiger. While the story of his ordeal is amazing by itself, the larger themes are universal—believing in the unbelievable, nature's incredible mystery and man's inescapable relationship with it, and God's impeccable timing, always showing up at the right place and time to meet the human need. This

is a great read, high-quality literature, and nurturing to the soul as well.

22. *Marriage of Sense and Soul, The* by Ken Wilber
Ken Wilber is one of the leading philosophers of science and spirituality today and has written several books that integrate the wisdom from many disparate disciplines into a comprehensive framework of reality. Many other leading philosophical thinkers look to Wilber's ideas to stimulate the continuing debate over what it all means. In this book, Wilber tackles the seemingly impossible task of integrating the core, genuine substance of both science and religion. While it remains to be seen whether the majority of humanity will ever agree to forthrightly reconsider cherished religious and scientific dogmas, Wilber's framework comprises as sane an approach to pursuing truth and meaning as I have seen anywhere. Along the way, Wilber treats the reader to an exposition of important premodern, modern, and postmodern philosophies that have gotten us to this point, as well as the way in which they have influenced the expression of the main "value spheres" of human existence—art, science, and morality. He also makes a strong case that both "valid science" and "valid religion" will soon need to replace their "bogus" and doctrinaire forms that are currently more widely held, if we are to continue to evolve. Wilbur achieves his goal of integrating the many layers of reality, the material and the nonmaterial, into a meaningful intellectual structure.

23. *Meditations of Marcus Aurelius, The* Translated by Gregory Hays
Marcus Aurelius was emperor of the Roman Empire from 161 AD to 180 AD and is considered one of the great philosopher-kings of all time. He professed a basic

conviction that the universe was a living, all-encompassing being in which natural order and harmony reigned. Being a Stoic, he believed that surrendering oneself to this divine intelligence and practicing detachment from worldly worries was the way to inner peace. During his rule, many serious problems beset the empire—famine, war, and failing public finances among them—so he wrote his *Meditations* as an apparent means of dealing with the stresses and fears he faced. There were twelve books in all, their insight now translated and condensed into this small volume. Upon discovering the *Meditations*, you will soon see how consistent these insights are with other universal, spiritual knowledge, and how applicable they still are in our modern world. I am fond of opening this book randomly to any page to see what pearl of wisdom I will find.

24. *Nature of Personal Reality (a Seth Book), The* by Jane Roberts
Jane Roberts channeled the nonphysical entity, Seth, for twenty years, beginning in the early 1960s. Her husband, Robert Butts, diligently recorded Seth's information into what became several books on the nature of individual and mass reality, dreams, healing, and more. In this book (my favorite), Seth tells us how we are continually creating our own experience of reality and teaches us how to become conscious of and own this process. Seth is a wonderful teacher who greatly expands our conceptual boundaries of the Universe and idea of what the Human Being is capable of accomplishing.

25. *No Boundary* by Ken Wilber
I would recommend this book to anyone setting off on the journey of self-discovery, or even to one who is well traveled but wants to get back to basics. Once again, Wilber brings his powerful intellect and personal experience

to his writing, but the result is a very straightforward, compact, and grounded survey of human consciousness, as well as a practical guide for reintegrating the self at each of the various levels of the psyche. What I found especially valuable were Wilber's descriptions of the illusions of time and separateness. Even though I have had direct experiences that pierced these illusions, and have read many of the wonderful books reviewed here that effectively describe the nature of unity consciousness, none does so quite as elegantly as this work. It came into my possession after all the others, but it still offered fresh moments of illumination where I felt that I really got what it meant to be in the Now better than I ever had before. It's a real catalyst for transformation.

26. *On Wings of Light* by Ronna Herman
This book is organized around the channelings of Archangel Michael, who comes through Ronna Herman. In addition to Ms. Herman's story, which is engrossing and, at the same time, consistent with others who channel, I found these teachings to be very powerful and inspiring. One of his messages touched me so much that I have presented it in Appendix A, below. It's called *Using The Universal Laws Of Manifestation,* and it really captures the divine, yet common sense, essence of this wisdom. I ordered this book at www.ronnastar.com.

27. *Path with Heart, A* by Jack Kornfield
The author uses many of his experiences to describe the landscape of the personal spiritual quest and the need to incorporate certain basic elements into whatever practice or discipline one might follow. Of particular interest is the informative discussion of meditation practice, particularly what to expect. It also discusses the true nature of human emotions, primarily how they contribute to suffering

and how to discern more subtle levels of their influence on our lives. An example is indifference, an ego-based emotion that often masquerades as detachment, an attribute that is truly spiritual. Writing from the heart with great compassion, Kornfield is someone with keen insights worth considering.

28. *Power of Intention, The* by Dr. Wayne Dyer
Dr. Dyer is the well-known author of many books, his earlier ones focusing on self-help and improvement, and the more recent ones gravitating toward spiritual empowerment. His latest work shows us how intention, both at a personal and universal level, is the engine that powers our experience of life. Most of the same points I make in this book Dr. Dyer drives home in his welcoming and inspirational style, using the power of intention as the thread that connects all we need to know about how to change our problematic lives into joyful ones. His message is that we are much more than we think we are, and that when we finally realize this truth, literally nothing is beyond our reach. He skillfully relates stories that illustrate how this power brought fulfillment into people's lives and how it can do so for you, too, if you let it in.

29. *Power of Now, The* by Eckhart Tolle
This book is another great place to start to get the essentials of spiritual growth and awakening. Tolle establishes in very direct language that we are much more than we think we are, and that we find the truth of this fact only in the present moment. He shows us how to practically apply the wisdom of the ages in our daily lives. This book came to me in early 2000, not long after it was published on a small scale. Four years later, it was on *The New York Times* bestseller list, largely by way of word of mouth. I

have read it many times to get back to basics whenever I feel the need, helping myself to the power of the wisdom it offers. This is another book I recommend to people when they need a short, condensed dose of spiritual understanding.

*30. Prophet's Way, The* by Thom Hartmann
This is a truly gripping and powerful story of the author's lifelong spiritual journey that follows the transformative relationship with his spritual teacher, an extrordinary man who ran a community for orphaned children in Germany. Hartmann's many experiences from all over the developing world, from Bogata to Bombay, show us the large scale suffering of great swaths of humanity and the urgent need for planetary transformation. His personal quest is one that gives us great insight into the possibilities for individual spiritual growth. It's full of adventure and at times unsettling, but hard to put down once you get going.

*31. Quantum Questions* Edited by Ken Wilber
Edited by contemporary philosopher Ken Wilber, this book contains a collection of writings from the pioneers of twentieth-century physics, particularly quantum theory, and demonstrates clearly that their curiosity about reality and their imagination ranged far beyond the physical world. All were mystics and philosophers, as well as great scientists. Besides the pleasure of exploring the eloquent writings of Einstein, Pauli, Schreodinger, Heisenberg, et al., Wilber's introduction to this anthology presents a fascinating model with which to approach the relationship, if any, between physical science and the realm of spirit.

## 32. *Rational Mysticism* by John Horgan

Mr. Horgan is a science journalist by trade, as well as a human being on a quest to find the essential nature of the mystical experience. He approaches this subject as an extended research project, interviewing leading lights in religious philosophy, neuroscience, experimental psychology, subatomic physics, and the study of psychoactive drugs. But, his comprehensively documented findings are anything but dry as he weaves his own spiritual experiences, and the personalities and experiences of his mentors, seamlessly into the material. The discussion on religious and scientific philosophies is good background for anyone who wants to know what the main explanations are for the meaning (or lack thereof) of it all. It's even more fascinating to see how these erudite arguments conflict more and more with each other as the book develops, and how the author forthrightly expresses his doubts and, at times, skepticism. He also includes lucid commentary about psychedelic drugs—their physiological effects, modern society's use of these agents for spiritual purposes, and an historical backdrop of drug/consciousness research, social impact, and commonly held misconceptions. For me, this book provided a deeper understanding of the major lines of thought concerning mystical states and reinforced even more how little the intellect can really know about, or explain, reality.

## 33. *Reflections on the Art of Living—A Joseph Campbell Companion*
Edited by Diane K. Osbon

Joseph Campbell was the foremost authority on the myths of the world, writing and teaching for decades on this subject. He wove together the common threads from the many cultural stories the peoples of the earth told themselves across the centuries to make sense out of their existence. This book is a great survey of mythological themes, the wisdom he derived from them and the lessons of his life experience. I have noticed that authors from various other fields of inquiry continually refer and build upon Campbell's ideas. His essential message is that, to be truly free, you must follow your heart.

34. *Seat of the Soul* by Gary Zukav
The author writes lovingly and with great insight about the characteristics of the human soul and its relationship to God. What's particularly interesting is that the author doesn't reveal anything about how he gained this knowledge, but it quickly becomes apparent that he speaks from the authority of one whose personal experience and revelation must have had a lot to do with it.

35. *Spiritual Emergency* Edited by Stanislav Grof and Christina Grof
Dr. Grof of has been acknowledged as one of the foremost researchers of human consciousness, first in his native Czechoslovakia, and then in the United States since the 1960s at Johns Hopkins University and other institutions. His wife has gone through several life-altering spiritual experiences. Together, they have organized a collection of writings by authors from different fields about the various ways spiritual awakening can upset one's life and equilibrium. A valuable resource for anyone, particularly a person who is having a difficult time awakening spiritually and who needs to understand more about what he or she is going through.

36. *Tao of Meditation* by Jou, Tsung Hwa
This treasure of a book explains the nature of meditation and spiritual enlightenment from the Chinese perspective of Tai Chi. It's very helpful in understanding what

meditation is, and isn't, and gives a practical guide to follow this ancient system. It also contains a highly lucid and intuitive description of the fourth dimension. The last part of the book is a fascinating account of the author's inner experiences. I ordered this book from Tuttle Publishing (800-526-2778 or www.tuttlepublishing.com).

37. *Tao of Physics, The* by Fritjof Kapra
A well-known explanation of physics for the layman, this book offers a unique comparison of scientific theory and experimental findings to Eastern spiritual wisdom, especially from the Buddhist and Hindu traditions. Kapra shows that physics is catching up with what the spiritualists have been saying for twenty-five hundred years, that form is really energy held in place by consciousness and is an illusion that is constantly changing.

38. *Toltecs of the New Millennium* by Victor Sanchez
This Mexican author was trained as an anthropologist. His fieldwork led him to a relationship of many years with the indigenous Wirrarika that live in the remote mountains of Mexico. Besides sharing the spiritual wisdom of the Wirrarika, and the engrossing description of their reality, he makes a compelling case for anti-anthropology. This is the answer to traditional anthropology, whose fundamental orientation is to classify and categorize what is observed into our system of knowledge. Instead, Sanchez asks us to recognize that self-evident knowledge of the world exists outside what is sanctioned by Western thought, and that for a valid inquiry, it must be investigated within its own frame of reference.

39. *World is As You Dream It, The* by John Perkins
The author was a successful international business

executive whose professional travels led him to live for extended periods of time in the rainforests of South America and Indonesia. He has written several books about his adventures, and especially his eventual transformation into a liaison between the indigenous Shuar people of the Ecuadorian Andes and the Western world. This book shares the shamanic wisdom of the Shuar, which he demonstrates modern society needs now more than ever. He also describes his guiding groups of Westerners to visit the Shuar, the events that transpire there, and how the visitors' lives are transformed.

40. *You Are the Answer* by Paul Tuttle

Mr. Tuttle, based in Washington State, is the founder of the Northwest Foundation for "A Course in Miracles", and the long-time channel of Raj. In 1982, he decided to sit quietly and listen for spiritual guidance, having exhausted all other methods of finding solutions to his overwhelming worldly problems. In a short time, he began having inter-dimensional conversations with an entity known as Raj, who began teaching him about the true nature of Being and Reality. Soon after, he found that Raj was actually Jesus, who didn't reveal his true identity initially, knowing how overwhelming this information would be. This book chronicles the first four months of these conversations and clearly shows the difficult choices Mr. Tuttle faced as spiritual expansion impinged upon him and his family to dramatically change their lives. Besides the powerful spiritual knowledge found in these pages, a window into what it's like to summon up the courage to trust into the unknown is opened.

Mr. Tuttle's book is actually available for downloading free of charge at the Northwest Foundation for "A Course in Miracles" (NWFFACIM) Web site www. nwffacim.org. This site also has channelings based on the teachings in *A Course in Miracles,* but goes well beyond, or at least makes it easier to understand in everyday language. Everything is covered, from personal problems to universal truths. A catalogue of past sessions is available directly over the Internet as downloads, all at no charge. They contain some of the most beautiful and inspirational teachings you will find anywhere. Several other resources are available in print form. The Web site is well done, especially considering that NWFFACIM depends completely on donations to do its work.

# Afterword

It's February 2009, about three years since I completed most of this book. After an initial attempt to find a publisher, I put the project aside, mainly to attend to the twin challenges of divorce after nineteen years of marriage and a layoff after a twenty-five-year career at the same company. Having moved through these events by following, as best I could, my own advice, I am ready to try again. My sense is that the making of *A World Within* had purpose, and if you are now reading it, then that purpose was evidently for it to be disseminated beyond a small circle of friends and family. I have also experienced the truth in what others have said about a work in progress becoming a living thing, with a growing need of its own to be embodied in the world.

As I went through the process of continually and lovingly crafting these words, I noticed that I, myself, was being helped as difficult circumstances, such as those mentioned above, waxed and waned in my life. At times, it felt almost as if the words came from someone else. While I can't say I directly channeled the book's contents, I had the strong impression that I was being guided from the way the information was organized and how it seemed to flow out of me. I have never written anything remotely similar before and certainly not in this style.

I continue practicing meditation, as well as many of the ways I mention in the book of dropping fear and extending love. Sometimes, I'm in the flow, so to speak, and sometimes, I'm not; but, on balance, I must say that this stuff really works. I notice many small miracles appearing in my awareness; money often turns up in unusual ways just when I need it, for example. Big ones, too, have been made directly possible, I believe, when I finally let go of situations that no longer were appropriate for me and trusted that I would be led to my greater good. Almost seamlessly, the relationship with my wonderful fiancée, Janet, began just as my divorce was finalized, and a very attractive job with a great company materialized soon after my old one ended. Other blessings always present are much more evident to me, particularly the many wonders of nature in all their splendor. But perhaps the biggest miracle of all is finally having performed the feat of breaking one hundred for a round of golf (even if it was only on a par seventy course and not from the back tees).

Generally speaking, I feel progressively more at ease with my life even as the normal helter-skelter of work, family, and the events of the world swirl around me. On an even deeper level, I am becoming more comfortable with the energy of Spirit and more willing to let go into it. I don't understand where it all goes from here; as you know by now, the adventure never ends. But if one ultimate secret of life is waiting to be discovered, it must be this: Learn to get off your own back; there's nothing wrong with you.

# Appendix A

## A Selected Channeling

I have included a channeled message below to provide you with a sense of what these very special communications are like. At the risk of being repetitious, I say again that you must compare any message from any source with your internal knowing to discern whether it rings true for you. At the same time, as objectively as possible, observe any biases that arise from old beliefs and conditioned habits, and ask if they are serving you well. For me, this brief message integrates beautifully many of the points made in the book.

### "Using The Universal Laws Of Manifestation" by Archangel Michael through Ronna Herman (26)

Beloved Masters of Light, today I would like to discuss with you the law of manifestation from a more mental and scientific point of view. We will set aside, for the moment, manifestation, and cocreation in harmony with Spirit as a part of your divine right and your spiritual heritage.

Many light workers are wondering why they cannot tap into the divine stream of wealth and abundance so they can accomplish their mission and fulfill their dreams. Many are still struggling to survive and meet their everyday obligations, while those who

189

operate from a standpoint of greed and power, very obviously in the third dimension, grow richer.

There are universal laws in force, neutral laws, that all must abide by, saints and sinners alike. There were great streams of energy sent forth, eons ago beyond remembering, by the Elohim, archangels, and cocreators of your universe at the direction of the Prime Creator. Any and all beings who carry within their soul a divine spark of the Creator have the ability to access and create with that electromagnetic or cosmic energy. But, you must know the rules and how to tap into that source and make it work for you.

First, you must have the right mind-set: you do not have to be spiritual, or good, or have lofty ideals; you can operate from a totally selfish point of view, even a desire to gain power or control of others ... the laws of manifestation will still work. If you would study or take a closer look at those who have amassed great wealth and power, you will see they have a vision, a belief in themselves and their ability to accomplish anything they desire. They begin by gaining the skills and knowledge necessary to make them experts in their field of endeavor. They spend as much energy and time as it takes to make their dreams a reality; they do not listen to any negative input from others and they do not doubt, even for a moment, their ability to accomplish what they desire and reach their goals. They draw to them those who have like interests and similar aspirations. They have their vision firmly planted in their mind and, day by day, moment by moment, they do whatever is necessary to bring that vision to fruition.

So what is the secret? Why do they succeed when many spiritual light workers have such difficulty creating enough abundance to live simply and gracefully so they can concentrate on fulfilling their spiritual mission and assisting others?

You are an electromagnetic force field, my beloved friends; you send out a frequency or vibrations, and those vibrations go forth and connect with like energy waves drawing to you more of the same. And so, if you have been saying affirmations and mantras day and night asking for wealth, if you talk continuously about what you want to accomplish when you have the funds, and yearn with all your heart and soul for abundance and it still is not forthcoming, why? Because you still have those old tapes lurking around in your subconscious mind that say: To be spiritual, I must deny everything in the material world. I must sacrifice my happiness and well-being in order to serve others (the old martyr complex). If I concentrate on my spiritual growth, God will provide … on and on.

One moment you are excited and feel you can conquer the world and manifest anything you desire, and the next, you begin to doubt yourself again. You say your affirmations for abundance and then allow your busy ego-mind to worry and fret day and night about paying your bills or getting a new car or a higher paying job. You begrudge paying taxes, or insurance, or the dentist, etc., instead of giving thanks and blessing the money that flows through your hands as you meet your obligations or exchange your earnings for the services of others.

Very few of you have the mind-set to handle great wealth, even if it did miraculously come to you. What would you do if suddenly you were given several million dollars? Would you hoard it? Would you be anxious about losing it or someone cheating you out of it? Or, would you spend it joyfully, creating your dreams and assisting others to create theirs, knowing that your abundance will keep flowing and there will always be enough to meet your needs and desires?

Now we are not talking about abundance making you happy or giving you a sense of fulfillment or about deserving it. Remember, we are talking about the impartial flow of universal substance, and I am sure you have noticed that many of those who are the wealthiest are some of the most miserable, bored, and unhappy individuals. But, you must give them credit; they do know how to tap into the universal source with their thoughts, desires, and determination. They never waver from their goals. They never let anything or anyone stop them or deter them from completing their mission. They envision, they desire, they believe, they act … therefore, they manifest.

You must begin to focus on the abundance you already have in your life … give thanks for it, be joyful about what you have and the good things in your life. Shift your consciousness away from what is wrong with yourself, those around you, and the world and begin to see what is right, beautiful, and wondrous. You must act as if you are entitled to all the beauty and abundance of the universe and that it is pouring forth in unlimited measure until it begins to happen. We are not saying you are to go out and spend funds that you do not have, but you can begin to see and enjoy the gifts that are available to you … many of which require no exchange of funds or energy.

Your thoughts are more powerful than you know; we keep emphasizing this, but you still allow your minds to ramble and to play, over and over, the thoughts of doubt, negativity, fear, guilt, etc., which make your affirmations ineffectual or cancel them out. One moment, you believe you can accomplish anything you desire, and the next, you are wallowing in self-doubt and pity. No matter how conscious you become spiritually, if you do not tap into that stream of consciousness with your mental body and mind that allows you to draw to you the energies of manifestation, you will never become a cocreator of abundance on the earth plane.

First, you must be very clear about what it is you want to manifest … feel the intensity within your soul-self, not your ego-self. Second, you must be sure that your desires are in harmony with your higher-self; you must surrender to the highest good for yourself and others, realizing that you cannot always see the larger picture, and also, you do not want to limit your Divine Presence as to how your dreams will be manifested. Then you are to listen to that inner voice of intuition—listen for guidance and expect miracles, and then take action as the path is revealed to you. When doubt arises, or your ego begins to play the old feelings of unworthiness or guilt, acknowledge and transmute the feelings and turn your thoughts to your goal.

Give thanks for the little miracles that take place, making way for greater and greater gifts to come your way. As you focus more on the positive aspects of your life, you are reinforcing these energies and drawing more of the same to you. You are creating a force field of love, abundance, and harmony which no one can disrupt or destroy—only you can do that. And, as you seek more awareness and spiritual harmony, you will find great joy and pleasure from your abundance for you will be in the flow of creation and in balance with all aspects of Universal Law. That is the secret, dear ones.

Now, let me explain another area of confusion and misinterpretation. It has been said by some that the earth has moved into the fourth dimension, and others say it is just now moving into the fourth dimension. Let me explain it this way; everything that manifests in the physical begins to manifest first in the etheric. Just as you are building your etheric light body, which will eventually create your physical light body, the same thing is happening with your planet earth. The earth's etheric body has moved into the fourth dimension, but the physical planet is still steeped and mired in the third-dimensional experience. However, as the three lower planes of the fourth dimension are cleared, this allows us greater access to and interaction with the earth and humanity and it allows those of you who have lifted your frequencies into the higher fourth dimensions to tap into that more rarified energy. It is as if you are living in a column of Light—higher frequencies that follow you wherever you go, creating a safe haven, or an island of protection and harmony, while those who still resonate with the lower densities continue in the illusion of chaos, pain and suffering.

As the earth accesses more and more of the higher frequencies (through the efforts of all of you wonderful, dedicated light workers) and this energy becomes anchored on the physical plane in greater and greater amounts, it will become increasingly more difficult to remain in the third-dimensional illusion—mentally, emotionally, and physically. And so, we are asking you, as Light Warriors, to strengthen your spiritual armor and resolve; to firmly envision your path and the goal you are seeking and to allow no one or no thing to divert you from your mission.

We know that it is difficult to overcome thoughts, habits, and traits that you have accumulated over thousands of years, but it is a time of new beginnings, a time to release your old limited viewpoints, doubts, and weaknesses. You are MASTERS; you are ascending into a new state of awareness, a new consciousness; you are evolving and returning to your perfected state of joy, balance, and harmony; where you will once again glow with the beauty of Spirit as it shines forth for all to see.

Dare to dream, dare to reach for the stars, dare to claim all that the Creator has promised you … it is yours for the taking, my beloved ones. But, remember, you must experience what you create; so together let us, once again, create an earth paradise where love, abundance, beauty, and harmony abound. I AM Archangel Michael, and I bring you these truths.

# Appendix B

## A Philosophy of Joy

Ideas that are congruent with much of the spiritual wisdom we have explored don't always have to be expressed in a serious way. I came across some very apt advice on how to live in the present moment, let joy into your life, and release fear, from an anonymous social philosopher on the Internet. To me, this is just another form of communication reminding us to drop the pretentiousness that ties us up in knots. I gladly present your thoughts on aging here, whoever you are, as a great approach to living life joyfully.

**Views on Aging Joyfully**

Do you realize that the only time in our lives when we like to get old is when we're kids?

If you're less than ten years old, you're so excited about aging that you think in fractions. "How old are you?" "I'm four and a half!" You're never thirty-six and a half. You're four and a half, going on five!

That's the key. You get into your teens, now they can't hold you back.

You jump to the next number, or even a few ahead. "How old are you?" "I'm gonna be sixteen!" You could be thirteen at the moment, but hey, you're gonna be sixteen!

And then, the greatest day of your life —you become twenty-one. Even the words sound like a ceremony: *You become twenty-one! Yes!*

But then you turn thirty. Oooohh, what happened there? Makes you sound like bad milk. He *turned*, we had to throw him out. There's no fun now, you're just a sour dumpling. What's wrong? What's changed?

You *become* twenty-one, you *turn* thirty, and then you're *pushing* forty. Whoa! Put on the brakes; it's all slipping away. Before you know it, you *reach* fifty, and your dreams are gone.

But wait! You *make it* to sixty. You didn't think you would!

So, you *become* twenty-one, *turn* thirty, *push* forty, *reach* fifty, and *make it* to sixty. You've built up so much speed that you *hit* seventy!

After that it's a day-by-day thing; you *hit* Wednesday! You get into your eighties, and every day is a complete cycle: you *reach* lunch; you *make it* to 4:30; you *hit* bedtime.

And it doesn't end there. Into the nineties, you start going backward: "I was *just* ninety-two."

Then a strange thing happens. If you make it over one hundred, you become a little kid again. "I'm one hundred and a half!"

May you all make it to a healthy one hundred and a half!!

**How to Stay Young**

1. Throw out nonessential numbers. This includes age, weight, and height. Let the doctor worry about them. That is why you pay him/her.

2. Keep only cheerful friends. The grouches pull you down.

3. Keep learning. Learn more about the computer, crafts, gardening—whatever. Never let the brain idle. "An idle mind is the devil's workshop." And the devil's name is Alzheimer's.

4. Enjoy the simple things.

5. Laugh often, long, and loud. Laugh until you gasp for breath.

6. The tears happen. Endure, grieve, and move on. The only person who is with us our entire life is our self. Be *alive* while you are alive.

7. Surround yourself with what you love, whether it's family, pets, keepsakes, music, plants, hobbies—whatever. Your home is your refuge.

8. Cherish your health. If it is good, preserve it. If it is unstable, improve it. If it is beyond what you can improve, get help.

9. Don't take guilt trips. Take a trip to the mall, to the next county, to a foreign country, but NOT to where the guilt is.

10. Tell the people you love that you love them, at every opportunity.

*Craig Bruce*

## And Always Remember:

Life is not measured by the number of breaths we take, but by the moments that take our breath away.

# Acknowledgments

This book stands on the shoulders of giants. The grandest of all is Spirit, who has shown me that truly nothing stands between us and who has helped me to find the North Star inside that was there all along. Next are the spiritual teachers and scientific visionaries whose wisdom has led me to understand that all is in order and as it should be. While I am deeply grateful to all of these sources for their insight, I wish to give special thanks to seven who have been particularly illuminating: Paul Tuttle and Raj, who make it clear that we are all in the process of awakening to our true state of perfection; Eckhart Tolle, who guides us firmly into the present moment; Neale Donald Walsh, who shares his healing conversations with a God of endless Love and no requirements of any kind; Lee Carroll and Kryon, who bring the incredible scale of Reality down to earth for us; Jane Roberts, Robert Butts, and Seth, who show us the unlimited power and freedom of human creativity; Dr. Stanislov Grof, who courageously brings his professional insights to his investigations of consciousness and spirituality, in spite of today's pervasive scientific materialism; and Jack Kornfield, who shows us how to live from the heart and grow spiritually while living in our complex culture. Last, but certainly not least, I thank Anne, Bernice, Bob, George, Janet, Judy, Laurie, Nancy, and Sheila for listening and for giving me invaluable feedback and help on the book.

# Permissions

Cover photo *Ocean Sunset* © 2007 Ken Buckner, www.doecreekgallery.com. Used by permission.

Paul Tuttle of the Northwest Foundation for "A Course in Miracles" who shared Raj's ideas and metaphors (www.nwffacim.org).

*Gates of Prayer* is © 1995 by the Central Conference of American Rabbis and is being used by permission, without fee.

Archangel Michael's message, *Using the Universal Laws of Manifestation,* through Ronna Herman (www.ronnastar.com).

Dr. David Lukoff of the Saybrook Graduate School for the classification of spiritual problems, and the DSM-IV definition of psychospiritual problems accepted in 1993, from the paper by Lukoff D., Lu F., Turner R. (2000) *From Spiritual Emergency to Spiritual Problem: The Transpersonal Roots of the New DSM-IV Category.*

Rumi's Poem at end of Chapter 7, translated by Shahram Shiva, from the book, *Hush, Don't Say Anything to God: Passionate Poems of Rumi.*

# Index

# Endnotes

## Preface
1  Lukoff D., Lu F., Turner R. (2000) *From Spiritual Emergency to Spiritual Problem: The Transpersonal Roots of the New DSM-IV Category.* http://www.sonoma.edu/psychology/os2db/lukoff1.html

## Chapter 2
2  *Gates of Prayer,* Central Conference of American Rabbis, New York, 1995.

## Chapter 4
3  See *A Joseph Campbell Companion* (reviewed in Chapter 9).
4  See *Diet For a New America* (reviewed in Chapter 9).
5  See Northwest Foundation for "A Course in Miracles" www.nwffacim.org

## Chapter 5
6  *With Toughness and Caring, a Novel Therapy Helps Tortured Souls,* New York Times, July 13, 2004.

## Chapter 6
7  *F. Capra, The Tao of Physics, p.70, Shambhala Publications, 1991. Chapter 4, The New Physics, also discusses the dimensions of the atom, pointing out that an atom the size of the dome in St. Peter's Cathedral in Rome, would have a nucleus the size of a grain of salt. The atom's "dome" is actually specs of dust (electrons) spinning around the grain of salt at very high speed.*
8  *B. Greene, The Fabric of the Cosmos, p. 88–92, Knopf, 2004.*
9  *B. Greene, The Fabric of the Cosmos, p. 47–50, Knopf, 2004.*
10 *B. Greene, The Fabric of the Cosmos, p. 77–81, Knopf, 2004.*
11 *Gates of Prayer,* Central Conference of American Rabbis, New York, 1995.

## Chapter 7

12 C. Casteneda, *The Power of Silence*, Washington Square Press, 1987.

13 *A Jewish Madonna? Is That a Mystery*, New York Times, June 18, 2004.

14 Jewish Virtual Library http://www.us-israel.org/jsource/Judaism/kabbalah.html - Zohar.

15 *The Lost Gospels*, Time, December 22, 2003.

16 Christian Mysticism http://www.kiskipby.org/links/spirit/mystics.htm.

17 Rumi Network http://www.rumi.net/rumi.html.

18 Rumi, translated by Shahram Shiva, from the book *Hush, Don't Say Anything to God: Passionate Poems of Rumi*. Poem on page 139

## Chapter 8

19 Lukoff D., Lu F., Turner R. (2000) *From Spiritual Emergency to Spiritual Problem: The Transpersonal Roots of the New DSM-IV Category*, http://www.sonoma.edu/psychology/os2db/lukoff1.html

20 The International Society for the Study of Dissociation http://www.issd.org/indexpage/FAQ2.htm - depers

21 St. John of the Cross http://www.newadvent.org/cathen/08480a.htm.

22 J. Campbell, *The Power of Myth*, Anchor Books, 1988.

Breinigsville, PA USA
16 September 2009
224073BV00008B/1/P